A VISI
THE MIJ

C000264132

The Second Goetheanum, in Dornach (Switzerland). Rudolf Steiner's masterpiece of organic architecture: home to the international Anthroposophical Society in its many aspects, to conferences and to many associated festivals of drama, music and eurythmy (a new art of movement).

A VISION FOR THE MILLENNIUM

Modern Spirituality and Cultural Renewal

An introduction to the work of RUDOLF STEINER

Selected and introduced by
Andrew Welburn

RUDOLF STEINER PRESS
LONDON

Rudolf Steiner Press
51 Queen Caroline Street
London W6 9QL

www.rudolfsteiner.co.uk

First English edition 1999
For information on the earlier English publications of the separate
chapters see p 131

Originally published in German in various volumes of the GA (*Rudolf
Steiner Gesamtausgabe* or Collected Works) by Rudolf Steiner Verlag,
Dornach: Chapter 1 in GA 136; chapter 2 in GA 191; chapter 3 in GA 118;
chapter 4 in GA 286; chapter 5 in GA 310; chapter 6 in GA 159; chapter 7
in GA 26. This authorized translation is published by kind permission of
the Rudolf Steiner Nachlassverwaltung, Dornach

A catalogue record for this book is available from the British Library

ISBN 1 85584 043 X

Cover design by Andrew Morgan. Cover photograph of the Goetheanum
by Ulrich Wolfgang Auer
Typeset by DP Photosetting, Aylesbury, Bucks.
Printed and bound by Cromwell Press Limited, Trowbridge, Wilts.

Contents

Foreword

'Could it be possible,' asks Rudolf Steiner in one of the lectures included in this book, 'for something of infinite importance to be now taking place without people being at all aware of it? Might not our contemporaries fail to have the slightest inkling of the most important happening in the world at the present time? It might well be so.'* And he refers back to the historical origins of Christianity to show that the profound events which changed the course of the world, changed the way people thought, felt and lived, were at first largely ignored, dismissed and their proponents despised by the representatives of the civilizations of the time.

Not that he means that such things might be happening again in a similar way. The matters of real significance, in fact, which are happening today are not repetitions of the past but rather anticipations of the future. That is why they are hard to see or to interpret, because we have not yet been able to grasp their implications or the scale of the events in which we are caught up. People have some sense of this, perhaps, as we pass the millennium and their thoughts turn, naturally enough, to the future that is about to start unrolling before us. Otherwise, we are so much involved with our day-to-day problems. Only a great turning-point suffices to raise our minds to the larger perspective. The modern age has few prophetic figures like those of the Bible, who challenged the world of their time and looked upon its doings *sub specie eternitatis*. But Rudolf Steiner is one of the exceptions. He is

---

* See Chapter 3, p. 66.

a great prophetic figure who insisted precisely on the dangers, as we gain increasing power and control over the world around us, of losing the larger view—and if he had been more heeded many of those issues of ecological and environmental magnitude would have been faced earlier, and understood more deeply. A philosopher who asserted human freedom, when it was being assailed by the scientific determinism which still seeks to impose itself today, he was also a religious and spiritual teacher who believed that the answers to humanity's changing problems could not lie in the past. Our age is actually the first where we can no longer look back to collective knowledge, which satisfied people in the past and which we can know to be safe. Modern individualism has broken that framework apart, and now as we have to take a further step it must either falter or reach for the kind of answers that Rudolf Steiner gave, and explored in depth in his 'wisdom of humanity' or anthroposophy. He himself was in no doubt that we cannot go back. Least of all could we find the spiritual values we miss by going back. 'Only if humanity looks forward will life again become spiritual ... Consciousness must become apocalyptic!'*

The end of the twentieth century and the new millennium that would follow were often the focus of Rudolf Steiner's lectures and ideas. So many of the global issues that loom over us as we cross the threshold of the year 2000 are prefigured in his writings and books that he more than anyone deserves the sobriquet 'Man of the Millennium'. But his attention was focused, as we approach that threshold, not so much on the stupendous outer struggles of the time (though he foresaw these too) but on the change in consciousness that has begun to fulfil his prophecies of the new inner reality that

---

* Rudolf Steiner, in his lecture cycle *Egyptian Myths and Mysteries* (New York 1987), pp. 35–36.

is dawning for humanity—if we take the opportunity that is offered. In his view, the advances of technology and science were not wrong; they are part and parcel of the freedom humanity has been given as its birthright. But they had not been matched by advances in the spiritual sphere. Religion was not wrong; but it was not adequate for people to try to cling on to broad religious truths in place of the detailed new moral perception that we need to bring knowledge of the spirit into the complexities of modern life. Science has certainly grasped the power to change the world as we know it, but that has left a need for a much deeper knowledge of human consciousness in its changing evolutionary development, so as to see where we really want to go with the power that we have. The assumption that human consciousness has always been the same is one that Steiner repeatedly challenges in these extracts, and throughout his life's work. For at root it is the wish that we can enjoy the fruits of the change that is happening around us without having to change ourselves. If we can suppose that the beliefs of the medieval religious mind can still be experienced validly, and with the same inner truth, today, without having to be dissolved and created anew out of the modern consciousness, then we can repose upon them while at the same time making use of the modern world's conveniences. Or we can have a consumer society that fantasizes about being Buddhist.

In face of the widespread temptation today to wish to turn back, or not to have to change, Rudolf Steiner trusts in the potential of spiritual truth to bring us to the answers our freedom really requires. If we go forward trusting to the spirit, to freedom, he promises us that we will find more than we know, whereas to stop or try to have it both ways can only, obviously, tear us apart. If we try to cling on to religion, and not discover it anew, we will be missing the new reality in the spiritual sphere which is the concomitant of the new awareness. It will be all very well to box in religious truths, defending them against the encroachment of science, so that we can still believe in the reality of the virgin birth, or the incarnation; but if we do not smelt all of this together with our consciousness of the deepest needs of the living environment around us, with the need to find ways of bringing people individually to discover the values that cannot any longer be handed down to them, to find bridges across the abyss that divide one human being from another, even (and often) in the closest proximity, we shall miss that greater reality which Rudolf Steiner describes as unfolding today. We shall miss the event he compares in importance to the founding of Christianity. For in the meeting of diverse individual visions, and of humanity with the morally perceived living universe to which individuals may commit themselves, and where they can again find belonging, can shine through the greater reality of the Second Coming of Christ.

The Second Coming cannot be received as dogma from the past but is to be found in the present, when we expand our spiritual awareness to the world around us. In place of the defensive or fundamentalist position of spiritual retreat, Rudolf Steiner is bold in taking spiritual concepts out into the world of nature, for example. He sees the cogency of natural science, but does not try to mix up spiritual and material truth. And he notices that our knowledge of nature and our power to manipulate it puts us in a position of moral responsibility. We have followed him in this recognition, somewhat belatedly, it is true, but now we find ourselves wondering what then we should do. Material knowledge tells us only that we have the power. Traditional religion has opted out of the whole development, telling us either that it is wrong as such or that it can have no bearing on spiritual truth. Few thinkers have had the straightforward courage to throw themselves directly into the crisis-situation, as does Rudolf

Steiner. Instead of drawing back, he asks us to deepen our awareness of the situation, so as to find the moral values we need out of our modern experience of nature. Instead of wondering what we should do, he asks us to become aware, to make ourselves open, freely, to the greater needs of the world and act to serve it, act as part of it. This will not mean giving up our own fulfilment, but understanding also what we ourselves are. So we need to intensify our perception of nature further, using all our human resources, to the point of moral awareness in the fashion he describes so beautifully in the lecture which forms the first selection below. And in this we will experience the activity of Christ—a redemptive activity, though one which we cannot find through the conventional ideas of older religious teaching. In reaching out to such deeper individual moral awareness, we touch already—perhaps not fully consciously—on the sphere of the Second Coming. And the knowledge of nature, Steiner shows, leads on to a spiritual knowledge that does not deny the advances of material thought—indeed, it belongs to the same trajectory, arises out of the issues posed to wider human experience by the methods of modern science.

Steiner's use of spiritual ideas to unfold the deeper consequences of the modern world and to give a new perspective to many of the familiar starting-points, whether in architecture, agriculture, education, care of the handicapped, etc., have been extraordinarily successful. He shows up the timidity of most twentieth-century spiritual thought, wary of tangling with the lions of materialism. In fact, from his spiritual point of departure, Steiner was one step ahead of many of the advances in twentieth-century thinking whether in the domain of developmental psychology, history of science, or the philosophy of religion. His bringing-to-bear of spiritual directness on the problems of education and architecture is also represented in the selections that follow. It is noticeable that, far from reaching out for some vague spiritual goal, he starts with the reality of teacher and child or human gesture in space that can be embodied in an artistic form. Instead of treating the child as raw material for the educative process, Steiner sees all that the child brings with it, its inner source of activity, already in development, absorbing and transforming everything that comes to it. Here is the reality of spirit and soul already at work in the child, which the educator can lovingly recognize and enter into rather than attempt to compel it into some pre-set form. Unless we are totally lacking in trust in the spirit, we need not fear that out of the child's amazing interest in things and love of activity nothing worth fostering will arise. Likewise a building such as the imposing sculptural masterpiece that is the centre of the Anthroposophical Society, which arose to pursue the initiatives of his life-work, is not imposed on the world around us. It is conceived by intensifying our sense of relationship to the living 'relief' of the earth's surface, which includes its vesture of growing plants. Yet it is an intensification that can only come about through the presence of a human artist, and the fulfilment he finds in artistic creation, even as a child left wholly to its own development without any parent or teacher would never learn to speak.

The freshness of Steiner's approach does not mean that he underestimated the difficulties or the struggles that always have to be fought. Indeed the earlier lectures selected here deal rather directly with the powers of resistance, or recalcitrance, of pride and illusion that beset all human ventures and colour all our relations with the world around us. Fulfilling the needs of the world around us and so—in the deepest sense—of ourselves can only be achieved when we know ourselves and consciously balance these distorting forces. Steiner's uncannily moving wooden sculpture of the Representative of Humanity, now housed in the Goetheanum, in Dornach (Switzerland), represents in its dynamic juxtaposition of figures the struggle and the inner victory that has constantly to be won. Again, the end of the twentieth century and the beginning of the new millennium was the time he expected the most severe of the spiritual struggles of mankind to come to a head. Yet his concern is not so much to 'refute' the materialism that so threatens human values today, or to deny its place in the world we have come to know. Far more important, from his perspective, is that we should understand how and why it has arisen and obtained such power. It is nonsense to expect materialistic thinking to go away in response to arguments. Rather we need to comprehend its place in the unfolding of human consciousness— and then we will be able to value it as one phase, even an important phase in our evolution, and no more. We will then be able to develop further, and move on.

Hence he advised that the exploring consciousness of the moral, free individual is the only weapon that can win this war. But in it, from the same direction as we may feel the renewed presence of Christ in the life-sphere of our earthly environment, we may feel the presence of a spiritual helper, an angelic fellow-fighter. Michael, the archangel who slays the dragon of materialistic thought, does not interfere with human freedom. But he is a power that can be realized through free individuals, and an inspirer of spiritual thoughts. Still too many people suppose that a spiritual perspective on life must mean withdrawing somehow from the world, once more transposing the outmoded religious patterns of the past unaltered into the present. The Michael-imagination, with which Rudolf Steiner allied himself and of which he spoke with increasing frequency in his later years, is the fullest representation of a characteristic exhibited by all of Steiner's work, represented in outline in the book that follows. For it shows us that the path to the spirit, and to the future, lies in taking part ever more deeply in the events and experiments of one's own time. Our time especially, as we turn the third millennium, will not disappoint us if we can follow Rudolf Steiner's way—the Michael path, and the path to renewed awareness of Christ.

Andrew Welburn

1. A Spiritual Perspective

The growth of environmental and ecological awareness is without doubt the most significant feature in the changing consciousness of our time.

Rudolf Steiner was far more than just the pioneer of the attitudes and ways of thought which have come to be seen as necessary in the crisis-situation we now face. In his 'spiritual science' he had already made the demand for greater awareness, had called for the kind of thinking that sees in terms of centuries, and even spoke of the 'planetarization of consciousness' as we try to define our new and, as he saw it, our creative role in relation to the world around us in the twentieth century. But reaching far beyond that, he is still the profoundest guide we have to the deeper meaning of the whole process of our ecological awakening.

We need above all to overcome the onlooker standpoint—the assumption that we can intervene in nature one-sidedly, without ourselves being affected. Our knowledge of nature needs to gain a moral quality. But the notion of nature that we have from modern scientific thought cannot furnish the ground for such a moral conception; and the general moral imperatives of traditional religious and ethical teaching are failing us in the new, complex world we face and have to deal with. Steiner describes how we have to find the new moral vision out of our changing relationship to nature, rediscovering its spiritual dimension not in large generalities but in the detail of our response to the world in which we live. Then instead of ourselves being reduced to nature, he argued, but by acting in relation to the spirit—the creative and moral order behind nature—we shall be in a position to heal the rift that has grown between human life and our wider setting in the universe.

By relating us to the spirit in nature, in fact, Steiner reveals our unique relationship of responsibility for the world, the fulfilment of our moral evolution, rather than making us only one further product of its material processes. Without turning back from our new-found freedom, his thought reveals the full meaning, and spiritual potential, of modern knowledge.

Behind the sense world, behind the world of human experience, there lies a world of spirit—a spiritual world. And just as we penetrate into the physical world through regarding it not only as a great unity, but as differentiated into individual plants, animals, minerals, peoples, persons—so can we specify the spiritual world into different classes of individual spiritual beings. So that in spiritual science we do not merely speak of a spiritual world, but of quite definite beings and forces standing behind our physical world.

What then do we include in the physical world? First let us be clear about that. As belonging to the physical world we reckon all that we can perceive with our senses, see with our eyes, hear with our ears, all that our hands can grasp. Further, we reckon as belonging to the physical world all that we can encompass with our thoughts in so far as these thoughts refer to external perception, to that which the physical world can say to us. In the physical world we must also include all that we, as human beings, do within it. It might easily make us pause and reflect when it is said that all that we as human beings do in the physical world forms part of that world, for we must admit that when we act in the physical world we bring down the spiritual into that world. People do not act merely according to the suggestions of physical impulses and passions, but also according to moral principles; our conduct, our actions, are influenced by morals. Certainly when we act morally, spiritual impulses play a part in our actions; but the field of action in which we act morally is, nevertheless, the physical world. Just as in our moral actions there is an interplay of spiritual impulses, even so do spiritual impulses permeate us through colours, sounds, warmth and cold, and through all sense impressions. The spiritual is in a sense always hidden from external perception, from that which external man knows and can do. It is the characteristic of the spiritual that man can only recognize it when he takes the trouble, at least to a small extent, to become other than he has been hitherto.

We work together in our groups and gatherings;* not only do we hear there certain truths which tell us that there are various worlds—that man consists of various principles or bodies, or whatever we like to call them, but by allowing all this to influence us, although we may not always notice it, our soul will gradually change to something different, even without our going through an esoteric development. What we learn through spiritual science makes our soul different from what it was before. Compare your feelings after you have taken part in the spiritual life of a working group for a few years, the way in which you feel and think, with the thoughts and feelings you had before, or with the way in which people think and feel who are not interested in spiritual science. Spiritual science does not merely signify the acquisition of knowledge; it signifies most pre-eminently an education, a self-education of our souls. We make ourselves different; we have other interests. When a man imbues himself with spiritual science, the habits of attention for this or for that subject which he developed during previous years alter. What

---

*From 1913 onward, Rudolf Steiner lectured extensively throughout Europe and fostered the study of spiritual knowledge within the organization of the Anthroposophical Society, which now has branches in most countries of the world.

interested him before interests him no longer; that which had no interest for him previously now begins to interest him in the highest degree. One ought not simply to say that only a person who has gone through esoteric development can attain to a connection with the spiritual world; esotericism does not begin with spiritual development. The moment we make any link with spiritual science with our whole heart, esotericism has already begun; our souls begin at once to be transformed. There then begins in us something resembling what would arise, let us say, in a being who had previously only been able to see light and darkness and who then, through a special and different organization of the eyes, begins to see colours. The whole world would appear different to such a being. We need only observe it, we need only realize it and we shall soon see that the whole world begins to have a different aspect when we have for a time gone through the self-education we can get in a study group on spiritual science. This self-education to a quite definite feeling with regard to the spiritual world, this self-education to a perception of what lies behind the physical facts, is a fruit of the spiritual-scientific movement in the world, and is the most important part of spiritual understanding. We should not believe that we can acquire a spiritual understanding by mere sentimentality, by simply repeating continually that we wish to permeate all our feelings with love. Other people, if they are good, wish to do that too; this would only be giving way to a sort of pride. Rather should we make it clear to ourselves how we can educate our feelings by letting the knowledge of the facts of a higher world influence us, and transforming our souls by means of this knowledge. This special manner of training the soul to a feeling for a higher world is what makes the spiritual scientist. Above all we need this understanding if we intend to speak about the things which are to be spoken about in this course of lectures.

He who, with trained spiritual sight, is able to see behind the physical facts finds at once—behind all that is spread out as colour, sound, as warmth, cold, all that is embodied in the laws of nature—beings, which are not revealed to the external senses, to the external intellect, but which lie behind the physical world. Then, as he penetrates further and further, he discovers, so to say, worlds with beings of an even higher order. If we wish to acquire an understanding of all that lies behind our sense world, then, in accordance with the special task that has been ascribed to me here, we must take as our real starting-point what we encounter first of all behind our sense world, as soon as we raise the very first veil which our sense-perception spreads over spiritual happenings. As a matter of fact, the world that reveals itself to the trained spiritual vision as the one lying next to us presents the greatest surprise to the present-day understanding, to the present power of comprehension. I am speaking to those who have to some extent accepted spiritual science, consequently I may take it for granted that you know that behind that which meets us externally as the human being, behind what we see with our eyes, touch with our hands and grasp with our understanding in ordinary anatomy or physiology concerning man—behind what we call the physical human body—we recognize a supersensible human principle coming immediately next to it. This first supersensible principle of man we call the etheric or life-body.

We will not today speak of still higher principles of human nature, but will only be clear that spiritual sight is able to look behind the physical body and to find there the etheric or life-body. Now spiritual sight can do something similar with regard to nature around us. Just as we can investigate man spiritually to see if there is not something more than his physical body, and then find the etheric body, so we can look with spiritual vision at external nature in her colours, forms,

sounds and kingdoms—in the mineral, the plant, the animal
and the human kingdoms, in so far as they meet us physically.
We then find that just as behind the physical body of man
there is a life-body, so we can also find a sort of etheric or life-
body behind the whole of physical nature. Only there is an
immense difference between the etheric body of all physical
nature and that of man. When spiritual vision is directed to
the etheric or life-body of man, it is seen as a unity, as a
connected structure, as one connected form or figure. When
spiritual vision penetrates all that external nature presents as
colour, form, mineral, plant or animal structures, it is discovered that in physical nature the etheric body is a plurality—something infinitely multiform. That is the great
difference; there is a single unitary being as etheric or life-
body in man—while there are many varied and differentiated
beings behind physical nature.

Now I must show you in what way we arrive at such an
assumption as that just made, namely, that there is an etheric
or life-body—strictly speaking an etheric or life-world—a
plurality, a multiplicity of differentiated beings, behind our
physical nature. To express how we can arrive at this, I can
clothe it in simple terms. We are more and more able to
recognize the etheric or life-world behind physical nature
when we begin to have a moral perception of the world lying
around us. What is meant by perceiving the whole world
morally? What does this imply? First of all, looking away
from the earth, if we direct our gaze into the ranges of cosmic
space, we are met by the blue sky. Suppose we do this on a
day in which no cloud, not even the faintest silver-white
cloudlet breaks the azure space of heaven. We look upwards
into this blue heaven spread out above us. Whether we
recognize it in the physical sense as something real or not,
does not signify; the point is the impression that this wide
stretch of the blue heavens makes upon us. Suppose that we

can yield ourselves up to this blue of the sky, and that we do
this with intensity for a long, long time; that we can so do it
that we forget all else that we know in life and all that is
around us in life. Suppose that we are able for one moment to
forget all the external impressions, all our memories, all the
cares and troubles of life, and can yield ourselves completely
to the single impression of the blue heavens. What I am now
saying to you can be experienced by every human soul if only
it will fulfil these necessary conditions; what I am telling you
can be a common human experience. Suppose a human soul
gazes in this way at nothing but the blue of the sky. A certain
moment then comes, a moment in which the blue sky ceases
to be blue—in which we no longer see anything which can in
human language be called blue. If at that moment when the
blue to us ceases to be blue, we turn our attention to our own
soul, we shall notice quite a special mood in it. The blue
disappears and, as it were, an infinity arises before us, and in
this infinity a quite definite mood in our soul. A quite definite
feeling, a quite definite perception pours itself into the
emptiness that arises where the blue had been before. If we
would give a name to this soul-perception, to that which
would soar out there into infinite distances, there is only one
word for it; it is a devout feeling in our soul, a feeling of pious
devotion to infinity. All the religious feelings in the evolution
of humanity have fundamentally a nuance which contains
within it what I have here called a pious devotion; the
impression of the blue vault of the heavens which stretches
above us has called up a religious feeling, a moral perception.
When within our souls the blue has disappeared, a moral
perception of the external world springs to life.

Let us now reflect upon another feeling by means of which
we can in another way attune ourselves in moral harmony
with external nature. When the trees are bursting into leaf
and the meadows are filled with green, let us fix our gaze

upon the green which in the most varied manner covers the
earth or meets us in the trees; and again we will do this in
such a way as to forget all the external impressions which can
affect our souls, and simply devote ourselves to that which in
external nature meets us as green. If once more we are so
circumstanced that we can yield ourselves to that which rises
up as the reality of green, we can carry this so far that the
green disappears for us in the same way as previously the
blue as blue disappeared. Here again we cannot say, 'a colour
is spread out before our sight', but (and I remark expressly
that I am telling you of things that everyone can experience
for himself if he fulfils the requisite conditions) the soul has
instead a peculiar feeling, which can be thus expressed: 'I
now understand what I experience when I think creatively,
when a thought springs up in me, when an idea strikes me. I
understand this now for the first time, I can only learn this
from the bursting forth of the green all around me. I begin to
understand the inmost parts of my soul through external
nature when the outer natural impression has disappeared
and in its place a moral impression is left. The green of the
plant tells me how I ought to feel within myself when my soul
is blessed with the power to think thoughts, to cherish ideas.'
Here again an external impression of nature is carried over
into a moral feeling.

Or again we may look at a wide stretch of white snow. In
the same way as in the description just given of the blue of the
sky and the green of earth's robe of vegetation, so this too can
set free within us a moral feeling for all that we call the
phenomenon of matter in the world. And if, in contemplation
of the white snow mantle, we can forget everything else, and
experience the whiteness, and then allow it to disappear, we
obtain an understanding of that which fills the earth as substance, as matter. We then feel matter living and weaving in
the world. And just as one can transform all external sight-

impressions into moral perceptions, so too can one transform impressions of sound into moral perceptions. Suppose we listen to a tone and then to its octave, and so attune our souls to this dual sound of a tonic note and its octave that we forget all the rest, eliminate all the rest and completely yield ourselves to these tones, it comes about at last that, instead of hearing these usual tones, our attention is directed from these and we no longer hear them. Then again we find that in our soul a moral feeling is set free. We begin then to have a spiritual understanding of what we experience when a wish lives within us that tries to lead us to something, and then our reason influences our wish. The concord of wish and reason, of thought and desire, as they live in the human soul, is perceived in the tone and its octave.

In like manner we might let the most varied sense-perceptions work upon us. We could in this way let all that we perceive in nature through our senses disappear, as it were, so that this sense-veil is removed; then moral perception of sympathy and antipathy would arise everywhere. If we accustom ourselves in this way to eliminate all that we see with our eyes, or hear with our ears, or that our hands grasp, or that our understanding (which is connected with the brain) comprehends—if we eliminate all that, and accustom ourselves, nevertheless, to stand before the world, then there works within us something deeper than the power of vision of our eyes, or the power of hearing with our ears, or the intellectual power of our brain-thinking; we then confront a deeper being of the external world. Then the vastness of Infinity so works upon us that we become imbued with a religious mood. Then does the green mantle of plants so work upon us that we feel and perceive in our inner being something spiritually bursting forth into bloom. Then does the white robe of snow so work upon us that by it we gain an understanding of what matter, of what substance is in the world; we grasp the world through something deeper within us than we had hitherto brought into play. And therefore in this way we come into touch with something deeper in the world itself. Then, as it were, the external veil of nature is drawn aside, and we enter a world which lies behind this external veil. Just as when we look behind the physical body of man we come to the etheric or life-body, so in this way we come into a region in which, gradually, manifold beings disclose themselves—those beings which live and work behind the mineral kingdom, the plant kingdom and the animal kingdom. The etheric world gradually appears before us, differentiated in its details.

In spiritual science, that which thus gradually appears before mankind in the way described has always been called the elemental world; and those spiritual beings which we meet with there, and of which we have spoken, are the elemental spirits that lie hidden behind all that constitutes the physical-sense-perceptible. I have already said that whereas the etheric body of man is a unity, that which we perceive as the etheric world of nature is a plurality, a multiplicity. How then can we, since what we perceive is something quite new, find it possible to describe something of what gradually impresses itself upon us from behind external nature? Well, we can do so if, by way of comparison, we make a connecting link with what is known. In the whole multiplicity that lies behind the physical world, we first find beings which present self-enclosed pictures to spiritual vision. In order to characterize what we first of all find there I must refer to something already known. We perceive self-enclosed pictures, beings with definite outline, of which we can say that they can be described according to their form or shape. These beings are one class of those which we first of all find behind the physical-sense world. A second class of beings which we find there we can only describe if we look away from that which

Rudolf Steiner's depiction of 'Elemental Beings' underlying the life of nature—even that part of nature normally said to be lifeless. (Pastel sketch.)

shows itself in set form, with a set figure, and employ the word metamorphosis—transformation. That is the second phenomenon that presents itself to spiritual vision. Beings that have definite forms belong to the one class; beings that actually change their shape every moment and, as soon as we meet them and think we have grasped them, immediately change into something else, so that we can only follow them if we make our souls mobile and receptive, belong to this second class. Spiritual vision actually only finds the first class of beings, which have quite a definite form, when (starting from such conditions as have already been described) it penetrates into the depths of the earth.

I have said that we must allow all that works on us in the external world to arouse a moral effect, such as has been described. We have brought forward by way of example how one can raise the blue of the heavens, the green of the plants, the whiteness of the snow into moral impressions. Let us now suppose that we penetrate into the inner part of the earth. When, let us say, we associate with miners, we reach the inner portion of the earth, at any rate we enter regions in which we cannot at first so school our eyes that our vision is transformed into a moral impression. But in our feeling we notice warmth, differentiated degrees of warmth. We must first feel this—that must be the physical impression of nature when we plunge into the realms of the earthly. If we keep in view these differences of warmth, these alternations of temperature, and all that otherwise works on our senses because we are underground, if we allow all this to work upon us, then thus through penetrating into the inner part of the earth, and feeling ourselves united with what is active there, we go through a definite experience. If we then leave out of count everything that produces an impression, if we exert ourselves while down there to feel nothing, not even the differences of warmth which were only for us a preparatory stage, if we try to see nothing, to hear nothing, but to let the impression so affect us that something moral issues from our soul, then there arises before our spiritual vision that class of creative nature-beings which, for the seer, are really active in everything belonging to the earth—especially in everything of the nature of metal—and which now present themselves to his imagination, to his imaginative knowledge, in sharply defined forms of the most varied kind. If, having had an esoteric training, and having at the same time a certain love of such things—it is especially important to have this here—a person makes acquaintance with miners and goes down into the mines, and below there can forget all external impressions, he will then feel rising up before his imagination the first class, as it were, of beings which create and weave behind all that is earthy, and especially in all that pertains to metals. I have not yet spoken today of how popular fairy-tales and folk legends have made use of all that, in a sense, is actually in existence. I should like first to give you the dry facts which offer themselves to spiritual vision. For according to the task set me, I must first go to work empirically—that is, I must give an account, first of all, of what we find in the various kingdoms of nature. This is how I understand the subject which was put before me.

Just as with spiritual vision we perceive in our imagination clearly outlined nature-beings, and in this way can have before us beings with settled form, for which we see outlines that we could sketch, so it is also possible for spiritual vision to have an impression of other beings standing immediately behind the veil of nature. If, let us say, on a day when the weather conditions are constantly changing, when, for instance, clouds form and rain falls, and when perhaps a mist rises from the surface of the earth, if on such a day we yield to such phenomena in the way already described so that we allow a moral feeling to take the place of a physical one, we may again have quite a distinct experience. Especially is this the case if we devote ourselves to the peculiar play of a body of water splashing in a waterfall and giving out clouds of spray, if we yield ourselves to the forming and dissolving mist and to the watery vapour filling the air and rising like smoke, or when we see the fine rain coming down, or feel a slight drizzle in the air. If we feel all this morally there appears a second class of beings, to which we can apply the word metamorphosis, transformation. This second class of beings we cannot draw, just as little as we can really paint lightning. We can only note a shape present for a moment, and the moment after everything is again changed. Thus there appear to us, as the second class of beings, those which are ever changing form, for which we can find a symbol for the imagination in the changing formations of the cloud.

But as spiritual seers we become acquainted in yet another way with these beings. When we observe the plants as they come forth from the earth in springtime, just when they put forth the first green shoots—not later, when they are getting ready to bear fruit—the spiritual seer perceives that those same beings which he discovered in the scattering, drifting, gathering vapours are surrounding and bathing the beings of the budding plants. So we can say that when we see the plants springing forth from the earth we see them everywhere bathed by such ever-changing beings as these. Then spiritual vision feels that that which weaves and hovers unseen over the buds of the plants is in some way concerned with what makes the plants push up out of the ground, draw forth from the ground. You see, ordinary physical science recognizes only the growth of the plants, only knows that the plants have an impelling power that forces them up from below. The seer, however, recognizes more than this in the case of the blossom. He recognizes around the young, sprouting plant changing, transforming beings which have, as it were, been released from the surrounding space and penetrate down-wards; they do not, like the physical principle of growth, merely pass from below upwards, but come from above downwards, and draw forth the plants from the ground. So in spring, when the earth is robing herself in green, to the seer it is as though nature-forces descending from the universe draw forth that which is within the earth, so that the inner part of the earth may become visible to the outer surrounding world, to the heavens. Something which is in unceasing motion hovers over the plant, and what is characteristic is that spiritual vision acquires a feeling that that which floats round the plants is the same as is present in the rarefied water, splashing up into vapour and rain. That, let us say, is the second class of nature-forces and nature-beings...

It is as though these spiritual beings had their jurisdiction, their territory, in these elements—just as man himself has his in the whole planet. Just as that is his home in the universe, so have these beings their territory in one or other of the elements mentioned. We have already drawn attention to the fact that for our earthly physical world, for the earth as a whole with its various kingdoms of nature, these different beings signify what the etheric body, or life-body, signifies for individual man. Only we have said that in man this life-body is a unity, whereas the etheric body of the earth consists of many, many such nature-spirits, which are, moreover, divided into four classes. The living co-operation of these nature-spirits is the etheric or life-body of the earth. Thus it is no unity, but multiplicity, plurality.

If we wish with spiritual vision to discern this etheric body of the earth, then—as was previously described—we must allow the physical world to influence us morally, thereby drawing aside the veil of the physical world. Then the etheric body of the earth, which lies directly behind this veil, becomes visible.

2. The Turn of the Millennium

Our most prevalent modes of thinking today not only fail to provide the kind of moral perception that Rudolf Steiner describes as necessary for the direct experience of the etheric or life-sphere; they actively impede it. Nor are they only to be found in advanced scientific and technological thought; they pervade the underlying attitudes of our culture. Many of Steiner's most 'apocalyptic' pronouncements refer to the life-and-death struggle which he foresaw, precisely at the turn of the millennium, would inevitably take place between these modes of thought, involving the whole destiny of mankind.

But we must be careful not to misunderstand him here. The way to overcome the dire consequences which result from following these modes of thought is to understand and use them rightly—not somehow to reject our history, and with it our individuality and freedom. Here again the traditional 'either-or' approach seemed to him to fall short of our over-whelming needs in the complexities of the coming millennium. Conventional religion, for example, recognizes a luciferic temptation and, whether or not it still makes reference to a fallen angel, we all know that the tendency towards self-glorification, towards setting ourselves up as all-knowing and beyond criticism, is a real power in our inner life! The Church long rejected science as man's attempt to set himself up in this way, instead of being content to accept through faith. And many today who are concerned at our plight still share the assumptions behind this traditional analysis. Why then has it never been able to change the impact of scientific thought, any more than the Church could stop science developing?

For Steiner, it is because this analysis sees only half the picture, and fails to see the real dangers involved. The real dangers come not from our self-assertion, but from the way that modern abstract, intellectual thinking paralyses our sense of self: it subjects us to the illusion of some absolute necessity imposed on us, inevitable as the working out of a formula. Hence we can forget that it is we who are constructing this world-picture. And hence we forget too that there are many other, enriching ways of engaging with the world that are just as real, and can put our world-picture in a different light. The power behind the rigid, spiritually paralysing attitude is just as potent as that behind the self-glorifying of the mind. Indeed our civilization is too often pitched from one to the other, from exultation at the power of science to the depressing meaninglessness it shows in answer to our human hopes. This second power Steiner calls ahrimanic, borrowing the name Ahriman from ancient myths but forging an idea that we need for the future. Both Lucifer and Ahriman are real forces in our inner life—and beyond that, they are real forces in all of evolution, since in their development all creatures need to elaborate their independence, assert themselves and attain supremacy at their right level, and likewise all things must be able to come to terms with their limitations, to recognize the unassimilable, the other. We must conceive of Lucifer and Ahrimen as cosmic beings, aspects of the universe in its evolution.

It is the evolutionary perspective which enables Steiner to transcend the 'either-or' morality of conventional religion. Both the powers have a role to play, despite the dangers that have led rather simplistically to outright condemnation or, conversely, to their unquestioning espousal! Lucifer has in large measure played a part in developing humanity's individualism. Ahriman poses more of the challenges of the present and the future. To let the ahrimanic dominate our thinking, even while it seems like the triumph of our intellectual achievement, will certainly destroy us as human beings.

By taking away any vestige of the human meaning in the world, it would lead to what Steiner foresees as the War of All against All. And because Ahriman is an intrinsic aspect of evolution, in some form that struggle, that ultimate War, must take place—but how, and when, may be influenced by the moral directing-power which we can, in reality, assert if we learn how to use the opposite powers in a balanced way, which is to say in freedom.

Most specific of Rudolf Steiner's prophecies is that concerning a human 'incarnation' of Ahriman at the time of the millennial struggle. He comes closest to describing what that means, perhaps, when he describes it as a human being or beings who have given up all for the realization of a purely ahrimanic intelligence '... since the brilliant, glittering, transcendent mind of an ahrimanic intelligence is more powerful than that in an individual human being—much, much more powerful ... an ahrimanic spirit can for a time take on embodiment, so that it is Ahriman who looks out of his eyes, Ahriman who waves his finger, Ahriman who blows his nose, Ahriman who walks.'

Ahriman's Incarnation

While as yet only a part of the third millennium of the post-Christian era has elapsed, there will be, in the West, an actual incarnation of Ahriman: Ahriman in the flesh. Humanity on earth cannot escape this incarnation of Ahriman. It will come inevitably. But what matters is that people shall find the right vantage-point from which to confront it.

Whenever preparation is being made for incarnations of this character, we must be alert to certain indicative trends in evolution. A being like Ahriman, who will incarnate in the

---

* Rudolf Steiner, *Karmic Relationships* Vol. III, P. 158 (London 1977).

West in time to come, prepares for this incarnation in advance. With a view to his incarnation on the earth, Ahriman guides certain forces in evolution in such a way that they may be of the greatest possible advantage to him. And evil would result were men to live on in a state of drowsy unawareness, unable to recognize certain phenomena in life as preparations for Ahriman's incarnation in the flesh. The right stand can be taken only by recognizing in one or another series of events the preparation that is being made by Ahriman for his earthly existence. And the time has now come for individual people to know which tendencies and events around them are machinations of Ahriman, helping him to prepare for his approaching incarnation.

It would undoubtedly be of the greatest benefit to Ahriman if he could succeed in preventing the vast majority of people from perceiving what would make for the true well-being, if the vast majority of mankind was to regard these preparations for the Ahriman incarnation as progressive and good for evolution. If Ahriman were able to slink into a humanity unaware of his coming, that would gladden him most of all. It is for this reason that the occurrences and trends in which Ahriman is working for his future incarnation must be brought to light.

One of the developments in which Ahriman's impulse is clearly evident is the spread of the belief that the mechanistic, mathematical conceptions inaugurated by Galileo, Copernicus and others explain what is happening in the cosmos. That is why anthroposophical spiritual science lays such stress upon the fact that *spirit* and *soul* must be discerned in the cosmos, not merely the mathematical, mechanistic laws put forward by Galileo and Copernicus as if the cosmos were some huge machine. It would augur success for Ahriman's temptings if people were to persist in merely calculating the revolutions of the heavenly bodies, in studying astrophysics for the sole purpose of ascertaining the material composition of the planets—an achievement of which the modern world is so proud. But woe betide if this Copernicanism is not confronted by the knowledge that the cosmos is permeated by soul and spirit. It is this knowledge that Ahriman, in preparing his earthly incarnation, wants to withhold from people. He would like to keep them so obtuse that they can grasp only the mathematical aspect of astronomy. Therefore he tempts many people to carry into effect their repugnance to knowledge concerning soul and spirit in the cosmos. That is only *one* of the forces of corruption poured by Ahriman into the souls of human beings. Another means of temptation connected with his incarnation—he also works in co-operation with the luciferic forces—another of his endeavours is to preserve the already widespread attitude that for the public welfare it is sufficient if the economic and material needs of people are provided for. Here we come to a point that is not willingly faced in modern life. Official science nowadays contributes nothing to real knowledge of the soul and spirit, for the methods adopted in the orthodox sciences are of value only for apprehending external nature, including the external constitution of man. Just think with what contempt the average citizen today regards anything that seems to him idealistic, anything that seems to be a path leading in any way to the spiritual. At heart he is always asking: 'What is the good of it? How will it help me to acquire this world's goods?' He sends his sons to a public school, having perhaps been to one himself; he sends them on to a university or institute of advanced studies. But all this is done merely in order to provide the foundations for a career, in other words, to provide the material means of livelihood.

And now think of the consequences of this. What numbers of people there are today who no longer value the spirit for the sake of the spirit or the soul for the sake of the soul! They are out to absorb from cultural life only what is regarded as 'useful'. This is a significant and mysterious factor in the life of modern humanity and one that must be lifted into the full light of consciousness...

Another tendency in modern life of benefit to Ahriman in preparing his incarnation is all that is so clearly in evidence in *nationalism.* Whatever can separate people into groups, whatever can alienate them from mutual understanding the whole world over and drive wedges between them strengthens Ahriman's impulse. In reality we should recognize the voice of Ahriman in what is so often proclaimed nowadays as a new ideal: 'Freedom of the peoples, even the smallest', and so forth. But blood-relationship has ceased to be a decisive factor, and if this outworn notion persists we shall be playing straight into the hands of Ahriman. His interests are promoted, too, by the fact that people are taken up with the most divergent shades of party opinions, of which the one can be justified as easily as the other. A socialist party programme and an anti-socialist programme can be supported by arguments of equal validity. And if people fail to realize that this kind of 'proof' lies so utterly on the surface that the No and the Yes can both be justified with our modern intelligence— useful as it is for natural science but not for a different kind of knowledge—if people do not realize that this intelligence lies entirely on the surface in spite of serving economic life so effectively, they will continue to apply it to social life and spiritual life irrespectively. One group will prove one thing, another its exact opposite, and as both proofs can be shown to be equally logical, hatred and bitterness—of which there is more than enough in the world—will be intensified. These trends too are exploited by Ahriman in preparation for his earthly incarnation.

Again, what will be of particular advantage to him is the short-sighted, narrow conception of the Gospels that is so prevalent today. You know how necessary it has become in our time to deepen understanding of the Gospels through spiritual science. But you also know how widespread is the notion that this is not fitting, that it is reprehensible to bring any real knowledge of the spirit or of the cosmos to bear upon the Gospels; it is said that the Gospels must be taken 'in all their simplicity', just as they stand. I am not going to raise the issue that we no longer possess the *true* Gospels. The translations are not faithful reproductions of the authentic Gospels, but I do not propose to go into this question now. I shall merely put before you the deeper fact, namely, that no true understanding of Christ can be reached by the simple, easygoing perusal of the Gospels beloved by most religious denominations and sects today. At the time of the Mystery of Golgotha and for a few centuries afterwards, a conception of the real Christ was still possible, because accounts handed down by tradition could be understood with the help of the pagan, luciferic wisdom. This wisdom has now disappeared, and what sects and denominations find in the Gospels does not lead people to the real Christ for whom we seek through spiritual science, but to an illusory picture, at most to a sublimated hallucination of Christ.*

The Gospels cannot lead to the real Christ unless they are illumined by spiritual science. Failing this illumination, the

---

* Rudolf Steiner discussed this and many other aspects of the Gospels from a spiritual-scientific perspective. See in particular his lecture-cycle *The Gospel of St John* (New York 1962); also Rudolf Steiner, *The Fifth Gospel* (London 1998). The 'luciferic' wisdom which originally enabled the cosmic nature of Christ to be understood refers to Gnosticism, a movement central in much of early Christianity though subsequently developing into an heretical 'alternative' to orthodoxy. Rudolf Steiner stressed its historical role in linking the ancient Mysteries to Christian thought; but he did not advocate return to its thought-forms when we strive for a cosmic-Christian understanding today: see 'Gnosis and Anthroposophy' in his *Anthroposophical Leading Thoughts* (London 1973) pp. 175–80.

Gospels as they stand give rise to what is no more than a hallucination of Christ's appearance in world history. This becomes very evident in the theology of our time. Why does modern theology so love to speak of the 'simple man of Nazareth' and to identify the Christ with Jesus of Nazareth— whom it regards as a man only a little more exalted than other great figures of history? It is because the possibility of finding the real Christ has been lost, and because what people glean from the Gospels leads to a hallucination, to a kind of illusion. An illusory conception of Christ is all that can be gleaned through the way in which the Gospels are read today—not the *reality* of Christ. In a certain sense this has actually dawned on the theologians and many of them are now describing Paul's experience on the way to Damascus as a 'vision'. They have come to the point of realizing that their way of studying the Gospels can lead only to a vision, to a hallucination. I am not saying that this vision is false or untrue, but that it is merely an *inner* experience, unconnected with the reality of the Christ Being. I do not use the word 'illusion' with the side-implication of falsity, but I wish only to stress that the Christ Being is here a subjective, inner experience, of the same character as a hallucination. If people could be brought to a standstill at this point, not pressing on to the real Christ but contenting themselves with an hallucination of Christ, Ahriman's aims would be immeasurably furthered.

The influence of the Gospels also leads to hallucinations when *one* Gospel alone is taken as the basis of belief. Truth to tell, this principle has been forestalled by the fact that we have been given *four* Gospels, representing four different aspects, and it does not do to take each single Gospel word-for-word on its own, when outwardly there are obvious contradictions. To take one single Gospel word-for-word and disregard the other three is actually dangerous. What you find in sects whose adherents swear by the literal content of the Gospel of St Luke alone or that of St John alone is an illusory conception arising from a certain dimming of consciousness. With the dimming of consciousness that inevitably occurs when the deeper content of the Gospels is not revealed, people would fall wholly into Ahriman's service, helping in a most effective way to prepare for his incarnation, and adopting towards him the very attitude he desires...

The unveiling of many more of the secrets of human life would be desirable at the present time if only there were greater willingness to face things frankly and objectively. For without the knowledge of certain facts of the kind indicated yesterday, it will not be possible for humanity to make progress either in the inner life or in the sphere of social life. Think only of something that is connected with the social problems we have recently been studying. It has been our aim to demonstrate the necessity for separating the spiritual life and also the political life, or life of rights, from the economic life. Our greatest concern is to create conditions throughout the world, or at least—for we cannot do more at present—to convince people of the necessity for conditions which would provide the foundation for a free spiritual life no longer dependent upon the other spheres of social life or as deeply entangled as it is today in the economic life on the one side and in the political life of the State on the other. Civilized mankind must either establish the independence of the spiritual life or face collapse—with the inevitable result of an Asiatic influence taking effect in the future.

Those who still do not recognize the gravity of the present situation in the world are also, in a certain respect, helping to prepare for Ahriman's incarnation. Many things in external life today bear witness to this. The ahrimanic incarnation will be greatly furthered if people fail to establish a free and independent spiritual life and allow it to remain entangled in the economic or political life. For the ahrimanic power has everything to gain by the spiritual life being even more closely intermingled with these other spheres. To the ahrimanic power a free spiritual life would denote a kind of darkness, and people's interest in it a burning, raging fire. The establishment of this free spiritual life is essential in order that the right attitude, the right relationship, may be adopted to Ahriman's incarnation in the future...

People do not grasp the reality, for reality can be grasped only when the necessity for spiritual knowledge and deep penetration into the nature of things is thoroughly understood. You are all familiar with the much quoted verse 'In the beginning was the Word, and the Word was with God, and the Word was a God'. Do people really take this lines in earnest? They utter them, but so often as mere phrases! No particular emphasis is laid on the tense of the verb: 'In the beginning *was* the Word, and the Word *was* with God, and the Word *was* a God' (John:1,1). 'Word' here must obviously have the meaning it bore in ancient Greece. It is not 'word' as understood today—word as mere sound—but it is the inner, spiritual reality. In either case, however, it is the imperfect tense that is employed. The implication therefore is: 'In the beginning the word *was*; but it is no longer'. Otherwise the sentence would run: 'Now *is* the Word; and the Word is *not* with God; it *was* with God, and a God *was* the Word but *is* so no longer'. This, moreover, is what stands in the Gospel of St John—otherwise, what would be the meaning of the words immediately following: 'And the Word was made flesh and dwelt among us'? This indicates a further evolution of the Word. 'Word' also means anything that man can acquire in the way of intellectual wisdom through his efforts and through his intelligence. But it must be quite clear to us that what 'word' denotes here is not really the goal for which mankind must strive at the present time or in the immediate future. To express what is now the goal, we should have to say: 'Let man seek for the Spirit that reveals itself in the Word; for the Spirit *is* with God, and the Spirit *is* a God.' Mankind must press on from the word to the spirit, to perception and knowledge of the spirit.

When I remind you of these first verses of the Gospel of St John, you will realize what little inclination there is today to take such things in earnest and to get beyond the arbitrary interpretations so often accepted in matters of the greatest moment. Human intelligence itself must be quickened and illumined by what is revealed in spiritual vision. Not that actual seership is essential; what matters is that the fruits of spiritual vision should be understood. I have repeatedly emphasized that today it is not the seer alone who can apprehend the truth of clairvoyant experience; this apprehension is within the power of everyone at the present time, because the spiritual capacities of people are sufficiently mature if they will but resolve to exercise them and are not too indolent to do so. But if the level befitting humanity is to be achieved, such things as were mentioned in the lecture yesterday must be taken in deep earnestness! I used a trivial example to show you how easy it is to be deluded by figures and numbers. Is there not a great deal of superstition where numbers are concerned? What can in some way be *counted* is accepted in science. Natural science loves to weigh, to compute, and social science loves statistics—again a matter of computation and reckoning. It will be difficult indeed for people to bring themselves to admit that all knowledge of the external world acquired through measure and number is so much delusion.

To measure—what does it mean, in reality? It means to compare something with a given dimension, be it length or volume. I can measure a line if I compare it with a line twice, three times, four times, etc. smaller:

In such measurements, no matter whether of lengths or surfaces or weights, the *qualitative* element is entirely lacking. The number 3 always remains the same, whether one is counting sheep, human beings or politicians! It is not a matter of the qualitative, but only of the quantum, the quantitative. The essential principle of volume and number is that the qualitative is left out of account. But for that very reason, all knowledge derived from the principles of volume and measure is illusion; and the fact which must be taken in all seriousness is that the moment we enter the world that can be weighed and measured, the world of space and time, we enter a world of illusion, a world that is nothing but a *fata Morgana* as long as we take it to be reality. It is the ideal of present-day thinking to experience in connection with all the things of the external world of space and time their spatial and temporal significance, whereas, in truth, what things signify in space and time is their external aspects only, and we must transcend space and time, penetrating to much deeper levels, if we are to reach the innermost truth, the innermost *being* of things. And so a future must come when people will be able to say: 'Yes, with my intelligence I can apprehend the external world in the way that is the ideal of natural science. But the vista thus presented to me is wholly ahrimanic.' This does not mean that natural science is to be ignored or put aside; it is the matter of realizing that this natural science leads only to the ahrimanic illusion...

It should be realized that just as external science becomes ahrimanic, the higher development of a man's inner nature becomes luciferic if he gives himself up to mystical experiences. The luciferic tendency wakens and becomes especially powerful in everyone who, without the self-training described in the book *How to Know Higher Worlds*,* sets about any mystical deepening of the impulses already inherent in his nature. The luciferic tendency shows itself in everyone who begins to brood over experiences of his inner life, and it is extremely powerful in present-day humanity. It takes effect in egoism of which most people are entirely unaware. One comes across so many today who are quite satisfied when they can say of something they have done that they have no cause for self-reproach, that they did it to the best of their knowledge and according to their conscience. That is an entirely luciferic attitude. For in what we do in life the point is not whether or not we have cause to reproach ourselves; what really matters is that we shall take things objectively, with complete detachment, and in accordance with the course of objective facts. And the majority of people today make no effort to achieve this objective understanding or to acquire knowledge of what is necessary for world evolution.

Therefore spiritual science must emphasize the following: that Ahriman is actually preparing for his incarnation; where we can recognize *how* he is preparing for it; and with what attitude it must be confronted. In such questions the point is not to say, 'We do this or that in order that we may have no cause for self-reproach,' but to learn to recognize the objective facts. We must come to know what is at work in the world, and act accordingly—for the world's sake.

It all amounts to this, that modern man only speaks truly of himself when he says that he hovers perpetually between two extremes: between the ahrimanic on the one side, where he is presented with an outer delusion, a *fata Morgana*, and, on the

---

* Rudolf Steiner, *How to Know Higher Worlds* (New York 1994).

other, the luciferic element within him which induces the tendency to illusions, hallucinations and the like. The ahrimanic tendencies in man today live themselves out in science, the luciferic tendencies in religion, while in art he swings between the one extreme and the other. In recent times the tendencies of some artists have been more luciferic—they are the Expressionists. The tendencies of the others have been more ahrimanic—they are the Impressionists. And then, vacillating between all this, there are the people who want to be neither the one nor the other, who do not rightly assess either the luciferic or the ahrimanic but want to avoid both. 'Ahriman—no!—*that* I must not, will not do, for it would take me into the realm of the ahrimanic; *that* I must not, will not do, for it would take me into the realm of the luciferic!' They want to be virtuous, avoiding both the ahrimanic and the luciferic.

But the truth of the matter is that Lucifer and Ahriman must be regarded as two scales of a balance and it is *we* who must hold the beam in equipoise.

And how can we train ourselves to do this? By permeating what takes ahrimanic form within us with a strongly luciferic element. What is it that arises in modern man in an ahrimanic form? It is his knowledge of the outer world. There is nothing more ahrimanic than this knowledge of the material world, for it is sheer illusion. Nevertheless if the *fata Morgana* that arises out of chemistry, out of physics, out of astronomy and the like can fill us with fiery enthusiasm and interest, then through our interest—which is itself luciferic—we can wrest from Ahriman what is his own.

That, however, is just what human beings have no desire to do; they find it irksome. And many people who flee from external, materialistic knowledge are misconceiving their task and preparing the best possible incarnation for Ahriman in earth-existence. Again, what wells up in man's inmost being today is very strongly luciferic. How can we train ourselves rightly in this direction? By diving into it with our ahrimanic nature, that is to say, by trying to avoid all illusions about our own inner life and impulses and observing *ourselves* just as we observe the outer world. Modern man must realize how urgent it is to educate himself in this way. Anyone who has an observant eye in these matters will often come across circumstances of which the following is an example.

A man tells him how indignant he is with countless human beings. He describes minutely how this or that in *a*, in *b*, in *c*, and so on, angers him. He has not an inkling that he is simply talking about his own characteristics. This peculiarity in human beings was never so widespread as it is today. And those who believe they are free of it are the greatest culprits. The essential is that man should approach his own inner nature with ahrimanic cold-bloodedness and dispassion. His inner nature is still fiery enough even when cooled down in this way! There is no need to fear that it will be over-cooled.

If the right stand is to be taken to Ahriman's future incarnation, people must become more objective where their own impulses are concerned, and far, far more subjective where the external world is concerned—not by introducing pictures of fantasy but by bringing interest, alert attention and devotion to the things of immediate life.

When people find one thing or another in outer life tedious, possibly because of the education they have received or because of other circumstances, the path which Ahriman wants to take for the benefit of his incarnation is greatly smoothed...

What I have just said may make you think that all these matters are very paradoxical. But in reality they are not. It is man who is paradoxical in his relationship to truth. What he must realize—and this is a dire necessity today—is that *he*, not the world, is at fault. Nothing does more to prepare the path for Ahriman's incarnation than to find this or that tedious, to consider oneself superior to one thing or another and refuse to enter into it. Again it is the same question of finding the point where everything is of interest. It is never a matter of a subjective rejection or acceptance of things, but of an objective recognition of the extent to which things are either luciferic or ahrimanic, with the result that the scales are over-weighted on the one side or the other.

To be interested in something does not mean that one considers it justifiable. It means simply that one develops an inner energy to get to grips with it and steer it into the right channel.

Ahriman or Christ?

The time when human progress was made possible through the constant refinement of the physical forces is already over. In the future, too, mankind will progress, but only through *spiritual* development, through development on a higher level than that of the process of the physical plane. People who rely entirely on the processes of the physical plane will find in them no source of satisfaction. An indication given in spiritual science a long time ago, in the lecture course on the Apocalypse, namely, that we are heading for the 'War of All against All', must from now onwards be grasped in all its significance and gravity; its implications must not remain in the realm of theory but also come to expression in the actions, the whole behaviour of mankind...

A task of mankind during the next phase of civilization will be to live towards the incarnation of Ahriman with such alert consciousness that this incarnation can actually serve to promote a higher, spiritual development, inasmuch as through Ahriman himself man will become aware of what can or, shall we say, can *not* be achieved by physical life alone. But people must go forward with full consciousness towards this incarnation of Ahriman and become more and more alert in every domain, in order to recognize with greater and greater clarity those trends in life which are leading towards this ahrimanic incarnation. People must learn from spiritual science to find the key to life and so be able to recognize and learn to control the currents leading towards the incarnation of Ahriman. It must be realized that Ahriman will live among human beings on the earth, but that in confronting him people will themselves determine what they may learn from him, what they may receive from him. This, however, they will not be able to do unless, from now onwards, they take control of certain spiritual and also unspiritual currents which otherwise are used by Ahriman for the purpose of leaving mankind as deeply unconscious as possible of his coming; then, one day, he will be able to appear on earth and overwhelm people, tempting and luring them to repudiate Earth evolution, thus preventing it from reaching its goal. To understand the whole process of which I have been speaking, it is essential to recognize the character of certain currents and influences—spiritual or reverse.

Do you not see the continually growing number of people at the present time who do not want any science of the spirit, any knowledge of the spiritual? Do you not see how numerous are the people to whom the old forces of religion no longer give any inner stimulus? Whether they go to church or not is a matter of complete indifference to large numbers of human beings nowadays. The old religious impulses mean nothing to them. But neither will they bring themselves to give a thought to what can stream into our civilization as new spiritual life. They resist it, reject it, regard it as folly, as something inconvenient; they will not allow themselves to have anything to do with it. But, you see, man as he lives on earth is veritably a unity. His spiritual nature cannot be separated from his physical nature; both work together as a unity between birth and death. And even if man does not receive the spiritual through his faculties of soul, the spiritual takes effect, nevertheless. Since the last third of the nineteenth century the spiritual has been streaming around us; it is streaming into earthly evolution. The spiritual is there in very truth—only people are not willing to receive it.

But even if they do not accept the spiritual, it is *there*! And what becomes of it? Paradoxical as it may seem—for much that is true seems paradoxical to the modern mind—in those people who refuse the spiritual and like eating and drinking best of all things in life, the spiritual streams unconsciously to them, into the process of eating and digestion. This is the secret of that march into materialism which began about the year 1840, or rather was then in active preparation. Those who do not receive the spiritual through their souls receive it today none the less; in eating and drinking they eat and drink the spirit. They are 'eaters' of the soul-and-spirit. And in this way the spirit that is streaming into Earth evolution passes over into the luciferic element, is conveyed to Lucifer. Thereby the luciferic power, which can then be of help to the ahrimanic power for its later incarnation, is constantly strengthened. This must come to the knowledge of those who admit the fact that in the future people will either receive spiritual knowledge consciously or consume the spirit unconsciously, thereby delivering it into the hands of the luciferic powers.

This stream of spirit-and-soul consumption is particularly encouraged by Ahriman because in this way he can lull mankind into greater and greater drowsiness, so that then, through his incarnation, he will be able to come among people and fall upon them unawares because they do not confront him consciously.

But Ahriman can also make direct preparation for his incarnation, and he does so. Certainly, human beings of our day also have a spiritual life, but it is purely intellectual, unconnected with the spiritual world. This purely intellectual life is becoming more and more widespread; at first it took effect mainly in the sciences, but now it is leading to mischiefs of every kind in social life as well. What is the essential character of this intellectual life?

This intellectual life has very little to do with the true interests of human beings! I ask you: how many teachers do you not see today passing in and out of higher and lower educational institutions without bringing any inner enthusiasm to their science but pursuing it merely as a means of livelihood? In such cases the interest of the soul is not directly linked with the actual pursuit. The same thing happens even at school. Think how much is learnt at the various stage of life without any real enthusiasm or interest, how external the intellectual life is becoming for many people who devote themselves to it! And how many there are today who are forced to produce a mass of intellectual material which is then preserved in libraries and, as spiritual life, is not truly alive!

Everything that is developing as intellectual life without being suffused by warmth of soul, without being quickened by enthusiasm, directly furthers the incarnation of Ahriman in a way that is after his own heart. It lulls people to sleep in the way I have described, so that its results are advantageous to Ahriman.

There are numerous other currents in the spiritual or unspiritual life which Ahriman can turn to his advantage. You have lately heard—and you are still hearing it—that national states, national empires, must be founded. A great deal is said about 'freedom of the individual peoples'. But the time for founding empires based on relationships of blood and race is past and over in the evolution of mankind. If an appeal is made today to national, racial and similar relationships, to relationships arising out of the intellect and not out of the spirit, then disharmony among mankind will be intensified. And it is this disharmony among mankind which the ahrimanic power can put to special use. Chauvinism, perverted patriotism in every form—this is the material from which Ahriman will build just what he needs.

But there are other things as well. Everywhere today we see parties being formed for one object or another. People nowadays have no discernment, nor do they desire to have it where party opinions and party programmes are concerned. With intellectual ingenuity, proof can be furnished in support of the most radically opposing theories. Very clever arguments can be used to prove the soundness of Leninism—but the same applies to directly contrary principles and also to what lies between the two extremes. An excellent case can be made out for every party programme, but the one who establishes the validity of the opposite programme is equally right. The intellectualism prevailing among people today is not capable of demonstrating the *inner* potentialities and values of anything. It can furnish proofs; but what is intellectually proved should not be regarded as of real value or efficacy in life. People oppose one another in parties because the soundness of every party opinion—at any rate the main party opinions—can be proved with equal justification. Our intellect remains at the surface-layer of understanding and does not penetrate to the deeper layer where the truth actually lies. This, too, must be fundamentally and thoroughly understood.

People today prefer to let their intellect remain on the surface and not to penetrate with deeper forces to those levels where the essential nature of things is disclosed. It is only necessary to look around a little, for even where it takes its most external form life often reveals the pitfalls of current predilections. People love numbers and figures in science, but they also love figures in the social sphere as well. Social science consists almost entirely of statistics. And from statistics, that is to say from figures, the weightiest conclusions are reached. Well, with figures too, anything can be proved and anything believed; for figures are not a means whereby the essential reality of things can be proved—they are simply a means of deception! Whenever one fails to look beyond figures to the *qualitative*, they can be utterly deceptive.

The following is an obvious example. There is, or at least there used to be, a great deal of argument about the nationality of the Macedonians. In the political life of the Balkan peninsula, much depended upon the statistics compiled there. The figures are of just as much value as those contained in other statistics. Whether statistics are compiled of wheat and rye production, or of the numbers of Greek, Serbian or Bulgarian nationals in Macedonia—in regard to what can be *proved* by these means it is all the same. From the figures quoted for the Greeks, for the Bulgarians, for the Serbians, very plausible conclusions can be drawn. But one can also have an eye for the qualitative element, and then one often finds it recorded that the father was Greek, one son was Bulgarian, another was Serbian. What is at the back of it you can puzzle out for yourselves! These statistics are taken as authoritative, whereas in this case they were compiled solely in support of party aims. It stands to reason that if the father is really a Greek, the two sons are also Greeks. But the procedure adopted there is just an example of many other things that are done with figures. Ahriman can achieve a great deal through figures and numbers used in this way as evidence of proof...

Hence there is a great deal in the spiritual and unspiritual currents of the present time of which people should be acutely aware, and determine their attitude of soul accordingly. Upon the ability and willingness to penetrate to the roots of such matters will depend the effect which the incarnation of Ahriman can have upon people, whether this incarnation will lead them to prevent the earth from reaching its goal or bring home to them the very limited significance of intellectual, unspiritual life. If people rightly take in hand the currents leading towards Ahriman, then simply through his incarnation in earthly life they will recognize the ahrimanic influence on the one side, and on the other its polar opposite—the luciferic influence. And then the very contrast between the ahrimanic and luciferic will enable them to perceive the third reality. People must consciously wrestle through to an understanding of this trinity of the Christian impulse, the ahrimanic and the luciferic influences; for without this consciousness they will not be able to go forward into the future with the prospect of achieving the goal of earth-existence.

Spiritual science must be taken in deep earnestness, for only so can it be rightly understood. It is not the outcome of any sectarian whim but something that has proceeded from the fundamental needs of human evolution. Those who recognize these needs cannot choose between whether they will or will not endeavour to foster spiritual science. On the contrary they will say to themselves: 'The whole physical and spiritual life of people must be illumined and pervaded by the conceptions of spiritual science!' ...

And here we come to a chapter that must not be withheld from the knowledge of modern humanity. If, in the future, humanity were to do nothing towards acquiring a new wisdom, then, unconsciously, the whole of culture would become ahrimanic, and it would be easy for the influences issuing from Ahriman's incarnation to permeate all civilization on the earth. Precautions must therefore be taken in regard to the streams by which the ahrimanic form of culture is furthered. What would be the result if people were to follow the strong inclination they have today to let things drift on as they are, without understanding and guiding into right channels those streams which lead to an ahrimanic culture? As soon as Ahriman incarnates at the destined time in the West, the whole of culture would be impregnated with his forces. What else would come in his train? Through certain stupendous arts he would bring to man all the clairvoyant knowledge which until then can be acquired only by dint of intense labour and effort. People could live on as materialists, they could eat and drink—as much as may be left after the war!—and there would be no need for any spiritual efforts. The ahrimanic streams would continue their unimpeded course. When Ahriman incarnates in the West at the appointed time, he would establish a great occult school for the practice of magic arts of the greatest grandeur, and what otherwise can be acquired only by strenuous effort would be poured over mankind.

Let it never be imagined that Ahriman will appear as a kind of hoaxer, playing mischievous tricks on human beings. No, indeed! Lovers of ease who refuse to have anything to do with spiritual science would fall prey to his magic, for by means of these stupendous magic arts he would be able to make great numbers of human beings into seers—but in such a way that the clairvoyance of each individual would be strictly differentiated. What one person would see a second and a third would not see. Confusion would prevail, and in spite of being made receptive to clairvoyant wisdom, people would inevitably fall into strife on account of the sheer diversity of their visions. Ultimately, however, they would all be satisfied with their own particular vision, for each of them would be able to see into the spiritual world. In this way all culture on the earth would fall prey to Ahriman. People would succumb to Ahriman simply through not having acquired by their own efforts what Ahriman is ready and able to give them. No more evil advice could be given than to say: 'Stay just as you are! Ahriman will make all of you clairvoyant if you so desire. And you *will* desire it because Ahriman's power will be very great.' But the result would be the establishment of Ahriman's kingdom on earth and the overthrow of everything achieved hitherto by human culture; all the disastrous tendencies unconsciously cherished by mankind today would take effect.

Our concern is that the wisdom of the future—a clairvoyant wisdom—shall be rescued from the clutches of Ahriman. Again let it be repeated that there is only *one* book of wisdom, not two kinds of wisdom. The issue is whether this wisdom is in the hands of Ahriman or of Christ. It cannot come into the hands of Christ unless people fight for it. And they can only fight for it by telling themselves that *by their own efforts* they must assimilate the content of spiritual science before the time of Ahriman's appearance on earth.

That, you see, is the cosmic task of spiritual science. It consists in preventing knowledge from becoming—or remaining—ahrimanic... The point is not whether people do or do not simply receive the wisdom of the future but whether they work upon it; and those who do must take upon themselves the solemn duty of saving earthly culture for Christ...

But remember that people today can prepare themselves to look into the spiritual world by apprehending with their healthy human reason what spiritual science has to offer. The effort applied in study that lets itself be guided by healthy human reason can be part of the struggle which leads eventually to vision of the spiritual world. Many tendencies will have to be overcome, but for people of today the fundamental difficulty is that when they want to understand spiritual science they have to battle against their own granite-like skulls. If the human skull were less hard, less granite-like, spiritual science would be far more widely accepted at the present time. Infinitely more effective than any philistine avoidance of the ahrimanic powers would be to battle against Ahriman through sincere, genuine study of the content of spiritual science. For then humanity would gradually come to perceive spiritually the danger that must otherwise befall the earth physically, of being rigidified into granite-like density.

And so it must be emphasized that the wisdom of the future can be attained only through privations, travail and pain; it must be attained by enduring the attendant sufferings of body and soul for the sake of the salvation of human evolution. Therefore the unwavering principle should be never to let oneself be deterred by suffering from the pursuit of this wisdom. So far as the external life of mankind is concerned, what is needed is that in the future the danger of the frozen rigidification—which to begin with would manifest in the moral sphere—shall be removed from the earth. But this can happen only if people envisage spiritually, feel inwardly and counter with their will what would otherwise become physical reality.

Ultimately, it is simply due to faint-heartedness that people today are unwilling to approach spiritual science. They are not conscious of this, but it is so, nevertheless; they are fearful of the difficulties that will have to be encountered on every hand. When people come to spiritual science they so often speak of the need for 'upliftment'. By this they usually mean a sense of comfort and inner well-being. But that cannot be offered, for it would simply lull them into stupor and draw them away from the light they need. What is essential is that from now onwards knowledge of the driving forces of evolution must not be withheld from mankind. It must be realized that in very truth the human being is

Rudolf Steiner and Edith Maryon, detail of the figure of Ahriman (left) from the large-scale wood-sculpture of The Representative of Humanity between Lucifer and Ahriman *which is now housed in the Goetheanum. Ahriman represents the threat of alienation and intellectual abstraction to the spiritual balance (freedom) of human beings. Below: plasticine artistic form for the head of Ahriman.*

balanced as it were between the luciferic and the ahrimanic powers, and that the Christ has become a companion of human beings, leading them, first, away from the battle with Lucifer, and then into the battle with Ahriman.

The evolution of humanity must be understood in the light of these facts.

3. The Etheric or Life-sphere and the New Awareness of Christ

The urgency with which Steiner speaks out concerning the dangers of one-sidedness in our modern life and, above all, in our ways of thinking, is matched only by the passion with which he spoke of the positive potential in that new form of awareness—our moral–spiritual perception of the life-sphere. For only there would we be able to experience the new revelation of Christ.

More than a new revelation, it is, as he describes it, a new kind of revelation. It is this aspect of his message which makes of Rudolf Steiner, in the end, something much more than just another religious prophet with a personal vision. For it is no longer right or possible for people merely to follow revealed truths. This is a revelation which will come to many, and finally to all who will receive it. Hence it is so vital that we all learn to recognize the spirit, and to recognize the tendencies of luciferic and ahrimanic which we need but which can distort our spiritual awareness. It will be for humanity to discover then in turn how to share those many individual aspects of the one vision. In the emergence of the spiritual-moral awareness lies the beginning of the Christ-experience of the future, which is described as beginning in its germinal form even in the twentieth century.

A key to understanding it is the vision of the rhythms of history. For behind the ebb and flow of the history of civilization stand the great outpourings of spirituality connected with the rhythms of the cosmos; it is these which made possible the varied forms of society and culture, which died away when new forms were needed or had emerged to replace them in a succeeding cultural epoch. Steiner refers to the five large epochal divisions that have arisen since the prehistoric, Atlantean time; and to even larger rhythms which have coloured spiritual life over aeons of time. Changes are coming about—or have already done so—on both these levels. The new Christ-awareness is our chance to be part of a rising wave, or rhythmic renewal of spirituality.

It is necessary first to look back, as often before, to earlier epochs in the evolution of humanity and of the earth. We are living now in the fifth epoch following the great Atlantean catastrophe. This epoch was preceded by the fourth, the Graeco-Latin epoch, when ideas and experiences of paramount importance of life on earth originated among the Greek and Latin people. This fourth epoch was preceded by the Chaldean-Babylonian-Assyrian-Egyptian period, this by the original Persian and this in turn by the ancient Indian. In a still more distant past we come to the great Atlantean catastrophe by which an ancient continent extending over the area of the present Atlantic Ocean was destroyed. This continent of ancient Atlantis was gradually swept away and the solid earth on which we are now living received its present configuration. In still earlier epochs preceding the Atlantean catastrophe, we come to the civilizations and forms of culture developed on Atlantis by the Atlantean races. And these conditions were preceded by still earlier ones.*

---

* See *Cosmic Memory* (New York 1971). The rise and fall of civilizations in the post-Atlantean world is related by Rudolf Steiner to the cosmic rhythm of the precession of the equinox through the signs of the zodiac in periods of 2,160 years: 7227 BC for the beginning of a prehistoric high culture in India; 5067 BC for prehistoric Iran (Persia); 2907 BC for the beginnings of Egyptian civilization; 747 BC for Greek culture; 1413 AD for the beginning of the modern ('fifth post-Atlantean') age. The sixth epoch to follow will commence around 3573 AD.

A survey of what is told by history—it does not, after all, go very far back—may easily give rise to the belief (although this is quite unfounded even for shorter periods) that conditions of existence on our earth were always the same as they are today. That is by no means so, for there have been fundamental changes—most marked of all in man's life of soul. The souls of those sitting here today were incarnated in bodies belonging to all these epochs of Earth evolution and they absorbed what it was possible to absorb in each of them. In each successive incarnation the soul has developed different faculties. Although during the Graeco-Latin epoch the difference was perhaps not quite as extreme, in the epoch of ancient Persia and even more so in that of ancient India our souls were entirely different from what they are today. They were equipped with faculties of another kind altogether in those olden times and lived under entirely different conditions. And now, in order that what follows may be thoroughly understood, we will visualize as clearly as possible the nature of our souls after the Atlantean catastrophe, when they were incarnated, let us say, in the bodies that could have existed on earth only at the time of the ancient Indian civilization-epoch. It must not be imagined that this civilization was to be found only in India itself—it was merely that in those days the Indian people were of prime importance. The forms of civilization differed all over the earth, but they bore the stamp of the instructions given for the ancient Indians by the leaders of humanity.

When thinking of the nature of our souls in that epoch it must be realized at once that knowledge of the kind possessed by people of the modern age was then quite impossible. There was as yet no consciousness of the self, no ego-consciousness as clear and distinct as that of today. The fact that he was an ego hardly entered a person's consciousness. True, the ego, the 'I', was already within man as a power, a force, but knowledge of the ego is not the same thing as the power of activity. Human beings lacked the inwardness belonging to their nature today, but instead of it they possessed faculties of quite another kind—faculties we have often referred to as those of ancient, shadowy clairvoyance.

When we study the human soul during waking life in those times we find that it did not really feel itself as an ego; an individual felt himself to be a member of his race or tribe, of his folk. In the sense that the hand is a limb or member of the body, the single 'I' or ego stood for the whole community of the racial stock and the folk. A person did not feel himself to be an individual 'I' as he does today; he experienced the ego as the folk-ego, the tribal ego. During the day he did not really know that he was a human being in the real sense. But when evening came and he went to sleep, his consciousness was not completely darkened, as it is today; the soul was able, during sleep, to be aware of spiritual facts—for example, of spiritual facts and happenings in its environment of which the dream today is a mere shadow, in most cases no longer representing their full reality. People had such perceptions at that time and they knew: there is indeed a spiritual world. The spiritual world was a reality to them, not as the result of logical reasoning, not through anything needing proof, but because every night, even if in dim, dreamlike consciousness, they were actually within the spiritual world. But that was not the essential. As well as sleeping and waking life, there were also intermediate states during which the person was neither completely asleep nor completely awake. In those states, ego-consciousness was diminished even more than by day, but on the other hand the perception of spiritual happenings, the dreamlike clairvoyance, was essentially stronger than at other times during the night. Thus there were intermediate states in which people had, it is true, no ego-consciousness, but were clairvoyant. In such states a person was as if transported, entirely unaware of his separate identity. He did not know 'I am a human being'. But he knew with certainty 'I am a member of a spiritual world, and I know that it is a reality for I behold it'. Such were the experiences of human souls in the days of ancient India. And in the Atlantean epoch this consciousness, this life in the spiritual world, was even clearer—indeed very, very much clearer. We therefore look back to an age when our souls were endowed with a dim, dreamlike clairvoyance which has faded away by degrees in the course of the evolution of mankind.

If our souls had remained at the stage of this ancient clairvoyance, we could not have acquired the individual ego-consciousness that is ours today; it would not have been possible for us to realize 'We are human'. We were obliged, so to speak, to exchange our consciousness of the spiritual world for ego-consciousness, 'I'-consciousness. In the future we shall have both at the same time; we shall all attain that state in which clairvoyance functions in the fullest sense while ego-consciousness is maintained intact—as can only occur today in one who has trodden the path of initiation. In the future it will again be possible for everyone to gaze into the spiritual world and yet to feel themselves a human being, an ego.

Picture to yourselves once more what has taken place. The soul has passed from incarnation to incarnation; once it was clairvoyant, then later on the consciousness of becoming an ego grew clearer and clearer and it was increasingly possible for the soul to form its own judgements. As long as a person still has clairvoyant vision of the spiritual world and does not feel himself to be an ego, he cannot form judgements or reason with the intellect. The latter faculty developed steadily but with every succeeding incarnation the old clairvoyance faded. The states in which man was able to gaze into the spiritual world became rarer; he penetrated more and more deeply into the physical plane, developed logical thinking and felt himself to be an ego.

We can therefore say that in very ancient times man was a spiritual being, for he lived in direct intercourse with other spiritual beings as their companion; he felt his kinship with beings to whom he can no longer look up today with normal senses. As well as the world immediately surrounding us there are, as we know, still other worlds, peopled by other spiritual beings. With his normal consciousness today man cannot see into these worlds. But in earlier times he lived in them, both during the night-consciousness of sleep and in the intermediate state of which we spoke. He lived within these worlds, in communication with these other beings. Normally, this is no longer possible for him today. He was, as it were, cast out of his home—the spiritual world—and with every new incarnation became more firmly established in this earthly world.

In the sanctuaries for the cultivation of the spiritual life, in domains of learning and in the sciences where such things were still known, account was taken of the fact that man had incarnated in these different epochs of Earth-evolution. People looked back to a very ancient epoch before the Atlantean catastrophe, when human beings lived in direct communication with the gods or spiritual beings, and when their inner life of feeling and sentient experience was naturally quite different. You can well imagine that this was so in an epoch when the soul was fully aware of being able to look up to the higher beings, knowing itself to be a member of that higher world. In considering these facts we will remind ourselves that we can learn to speak and think today if we grow up among human beings, for such faculties can be acquired only through contact with people. If a child were to be put on some lonely island today and grew up without having any contact with human beings, it would not develop the faculties of thinking and speaking.

This shows that the evolution of any being is to some extent dependent upon the species of beings among whom it grows up and lives. That this has an effect upon evolution can be observed in the case of animals. It is well known that if dogs are removed from conditions where they are in contact with human beings to places where they have no such contact, they forget how to bark. As a rule the descendants of such dogs cannot bark at all. Something does, then, depend upon the kind of beings among which a being grows up. You can therefore imagine that for the same souls to live among modern people on the physical plane is a different matter from having lived at an earlier time among spiritual beings in a spiritual world into which normal vision today does not penetrate. The impulses man developed when living among people and those he developed when living among gods were quite different.

Higher knowledge has always recognized these things, has always looked back to that ancient time when people were in direct contact with divine-spiritual beings. And the effect of this contact was that the soul felt itself a member of the divine-spiritual world. But this also engendered impulses and forces in the soul that were still of a divine-spiritual nature— divine-spiritual in quite another sense from that which applies to the forces of the soul today. When the soul felt itself a member of the higher world, there spoke out of this soul a will that also sprang from the divine-spiritual world—a will of which it might rightly be said that it was inspired, because the soul was living among gods.

Higher knowledge speaks of this age when man was still united with the divine-spiritual beings as the Golden Age, or *Krita Yuga.* It is an age of great antiquity, the most important period of which actually preceded the Atlantean catastrophe.

Then came an age when people no longer felt their connection with the divine-spiritual world as strongly as during *Krita Yuga*, when they no longer felt that their impulses were determined by their life with the gods, when their vision of the spirit and the soul was already clouded. Nevertheless, there still remained in them a memory of their life with the spiritual beings and the gods.

This memory was particularly distinct in ancient India. It was very easy in those days to speak about spiritual things; one could have directed people's attention to the outer, physically perceptible world and yet regard it as *maya* or illusion, because people had not been having these physical perceptions for so very long. So it was in ancient India. Souls then living no longer beheld the gods themselves, but they still beheld spiritual facts and happenings and spiritual beings of lower ranks. Only a comparatively small number of human beings were still able to behold the sublime spiritual beings, and even for these people the former living communion with the gods was already much less intense. The will-impulses from the divine-spiritual world had already disappeared. Nevertheless, a glimpse into spiritual facts and happenings was still possible, at all events in certain states of consciousness—in sleep, and in those intermediate states to which reference has been made.

The most important facts of this spiritual world, however, which in earlier times had been experienced as immediate reality, were now there in the form of a kind of knowledge of truth, as something that the soul still knew with certainty but which was now operative only in the form of knowledge, as a truth. People still lived in the spiritual world, but in this later age the realization of its existence was not as strong as it had formerly been. This period is called the Silver Age, or *Trita Yuga.*

Then came the epoch of those incarnations when man's

vision was more and more shut off from the spiritual world,
when his whole nature was directed to the outer sense-world
and firmly consolidated in that world; inner ego-consciousness, consciousness of being human, became more and more
definite and distinct. This is the Bronze Age, or *Dvapara
Yuga.* Man's knowledge of the spiritual world was no longer
as sublime or direct as in earlier times, but something at least
had remained in humanity. It was as if in people of the
present day who have reached a certain age there were to
remain something of the jubilance of youth; this is past and
over but it has been experienced and known and a person can
speak of it as something with which he is familiar. Thus the
souls of that age were still in some degree familiar with
experiences leading to the spiritual worlds. That is the
essential characteristic of *Dvapara Yuga.*

But then came another age, an age when even this
degree of familiarity with the spiritual world ceased, when
the doors of the spiritual world closed. People's vision was
more and more confined to the outer material world and to
the intellect which elaborates the sense-impressions, so that
the only remaining possibility was to reflect about the spiritual world—which is the most unsatisfactory way of acquiring knowledge of it. What people now actually knew from
their own experience was the material-physical world. If
they desired to know something about the spiritual world,
this was possible only through reflection. It is the age when
humanity was most lacking in spirituality and therefore
established itself firmly in the material world. This was
necessary in order that it might be able by degrees to
develop consciousness of self to its highest point, for only
through the sturdy resistance of the outer world could man
learn to distinguish himself from the world and experience
himself as an individual. This age is called *Kali Yuga,* or
the Dark Age.

I emphasize that these designations—*Krita Yuga*, for example—can also be applied to longer epochs, for before the Golden Age man experienced and participated in still higher worlds; hence all those earlier ages could be embraced by this name. But if, so to speak, demands are kept moderate and one is satisfied with the range of spiritual experience described, the periods can be divided in the way indicated. Definite time periods can be given for all such epochs. True, evolution progresses slowly and by degrees, but there are certain boundary-lines of which it can be said that prior to them such-and-such conditions of life and of consciousness predominated, and subsequently others.

Accordingly, in the sense first spoken of, *Kali Yuga* began approximately in the year 3101 BC. Thus we realize that our souls have appeared repeatedly on the earth in new incarnations, in the course of which man's vision has been more and more shut off from the spiritual world and therefore increasingly restricted to the outer world of the senses. We realize, too, that with every incarnation our souls enter into new conditions in which there are always new things to be learnt. What we can achieve in *Kali Yuga* is to establish and consolidate our ego-consciousness. This was not previously possible, for we had first to be endowed with the ego.

If in some incarnation souls have failed to take in what that particular epoch has to give, it is very difficult for the loss to be made good in later epochs. Such souls must wait a long time until the loss can in some respect be counterbalanced. But no reliance should be placed upon such a possibility.

We will therefore picture to ourselves that the result of the doors being closed against the spiritual world was of fundamental and essential importance. This was also the epoch of John the Baptist, of Christ Himself on earth. In that epoch, when 3,100 years of the Dark Age had already elapsed, a fact of salient importance was that all human beings then living had already been incarnated several times—once or twice at the very least—in the Dark Age. Ego-consciousness had been firmly established; memory of the spiritual world had faded away, and if people did not desire to lose their connection with the spiritual world entirely it was essential for them to learn to experience within the ego the reality of the spiritual world. The ego must have developed to the stage where it could be certain—in its inmost core at least—that there is a spiritual world, and that there are higher spiritual beings. The ego must have made itself capable of feeling, of believing in, the spiritual world.

If in the days of Christ Jesus someone had voiced the truth in regard to the conditions then prevailing, he might have said: 'In earlier times people could experience the kingdom of heaven while they were outside their ego in those spiritual distances reached when out of the body. Humanity had then to experience the kingdoms of heaven, the kingdoms of the spiritual world, far away from the ego. This is no longer possible, for man's nature has changed so greatly that these kingdoms must be experienced within the ego itself; the kingdoms of heaven have come so near to man that they work into his very ego. And it was this that was proclaimed by John the Baptist: The kingdoms of heaven are at hand!—that is to say, they have drawn near to the ego. Previously they were outside man, but now they are near and man must grasp them in the very core of his being, in the ego. And because in this Dark Age, in *Kali Yuga*, man could no longer go forth from the physical into the spiritual world, it was necessary for the Divine Being, Christ, to come down into the physical world.' Christ's descent into a man of flesh, into Jesus of Nazareth, was necessary in order that through beholding the life and deeds of Christ on the physical plane it might become possible for mankind to be linked, in the physical body, with the kingdoms of heaven, with the spiritual world. And so Christ's sojourn on earth took place during a period in the middle of *Kali Yuga*, the Dark Age, when people who were not living in a state of dull insensibility but understood the nature of the times could realize: The descent of God to men is necessary in order that a lost connection with the spiritual world may be established once again.

If at that time no human beings had been able to find a living link with Christ in their hearts and souls, the connection with the spiritual worlds would gradually have been lost; the kingdoms of heaven would not have been received into the egos of mankind. It might well have happened that if all human beings living at that crucial point of time had persisted in remaining in darkness, an event of such momentous significance would have passed them by unnoticed. The souls of people would have withered, gone to waste, decayed. True, even without Christ they would have continued to incarnate for some time still, but they would not have been able to implant in the ego the power that would have enabled them to find the link with the kingdoms of heaven. The event of the appearance of Christ on the earth might everywhere have passed unnoticed—as it did, for example, in Rome. It was alleged in Rome that a sect of sinful people were living in some out-of-the-way, sordid alley, and that among them was a wicked spirit calling himself Jesus of Nazareth and inciting them by his preaching to all kinds of villainous deeds. At a certain period that was all that was known in Rome of Christ! And you may possibly also be aware that Tacitus, the great Roman historian, wrote in a similar vein about a hundred years after the events in Palestine.

Thus it was by no means universally realized that something of supreme importance had taken place: that the Divine Light had shone into the darkness of earth and that it was now possible for people to be brought safely through *Kali*

Rudolf Steiner and Edith Maryon, The Representative of Humanity between Lucifer and Ahriman *(Goetheanum, Dornach). The central figure achieves mastery over the contrary powers through spiritual strength and suffering, and may be seen as a Christfigure. The seraphic Spirit of Humour (top left) suggests transcendence and release.*

Yuga. The possibility of further evolution for humanity was ensured because there were certain souls who understood what was at stake at that point of time and knew what it signified that Christ had been upon earth.

If you were to transfer yourselves in thought to that time, you would realize that it was quite possible to live without knowing anything at all of the advent of Christ Jesus on the physical plane—it was quite possible to live on earth without having any consciousness of this most momentous event.

Would it not also be possible today for something of infinite importance to take place without people being aware of it? Might not our contemporaries fail to have the slightest inkling of the most important happening in the world at the present time? It might well be so. For something of supreme importance is taking place, although it is perceptible only to the eyes of spirit. There is a great deal of talk about periods of transition; we ourselves are actually living in a very important one. And its importance lies in the fact that the Dark Age has run its course and a new age is beginning, when slowly and by degrees the souls of human beings will change and new faculties will be developed.

The fact that the vast majority of people are entirely unaware of this need not be the cause of surprise, for it was the same when the Christ Event took place at the beginning of our era. *Kali Yuga* came to an end in the year 1899 and we have now to live on into a new age. What is beginning is slowly preparing people for new faculties of soul.

The first indications of these new faculties will be noticeable in isolated souls comparatively soon now, and they will become more clearly apparent in the middle of the thirties of this century, approximately in the period between 1930 and 1940. The years 1933, 1935 and 1937 will be particularly important. Very special faculties will then reveal themselves in human beings as natural gifts. Great changes will take place during this period and biblical prophecies will be fulfilled. Everything will change for souls who are living on earth and also for those who are no longer in physical bodies. Whatever their realm of existence, souls are on the way to possessing entirely new faculties. Everything is changing—but the happening of supreme importance in our time is a deeply incisive transformation of the faculties of the human soul.

Kali Yuga is over and the souls of human beings are now beginning to develop new faculties. These faculties—because this is the purpose of the epoch—will of themselves draw forth from souls certain powers of clairvoyance which during *Kali Yuga* had necessarily to be submerged in the realm of the unconscious. A number of souls will experience the strange condition of having ego-consciousness but at the same time the feeling of living in a world essentially different from the world known to their ordinary consciousness. The experience will be shadowy, like a divination, as though an operation had been performed on one born blind. Through what we call esoteric training these clairvoyant faculties will be attained in a far better form. But because human beings progress, they will appear in mankind in their very earliest beginnings, in their most elementary stages, through the natural process of evolution.

But it might very easily happen—indeed, far more easily now than at any earlier time—that people would prove incapable of grasping this event of such supreme importance for humanity, incapable of realizing that this denotes an actual glimpse into a spiritual world, although still shadowy and dim. There might, for example, be so much wickedness, so much materialism on the earth that the majority of people would show not the slightest understanding, and regard those who have this clairvoyance as lunatics, shutting them up in asylums together with those whose minds are obviously deranged. This point of time might pass people by without leaving a trace, although today we too are letting the call of John the Baptist, the forerunner of Christ, and of Christ Himself, again resound: A new epoch is at hand when the souls of human beings must take a step upward into the kingdoms of heaven.

The great event might very easily pass without being understood by people. If between the years 1930 and 1940 the materialists were to say triumphantly, 'True, there have been a number of fools but no sign whatever of the expected great event,' this would not in the least disprove what has been said. But if the materialists were to win the day and mankind were to overlook these happenings altogether, it would be a dire misfortune. Even if people should prove incapable of perceiving them, great things will come to pass.

One is that it will be possible for people to acquire the new faculty of perception in the etheric world—a certain number to begin with, and they will be followed by more and more others, for mankind will have 2,500 years during which to develop these faculties to greater and greater perfection. This opportunity must not be missed. If it were, this would be a tragic misfortune and mankind would then be obliged to wait until a later epoch in order to retrieve the lost opportunity and subsequently to develop the new faculty. This faculty will consist in persons being able to see in their environment something of the etheric world which hitherto they have not normally been able to see. Mankind now sees only the human physical body, but then they will be able to see the etheric body at least as a shadowy picture and also to perceive the connection between deeper happenings in the etheric world. They will have pictures and premonitions of happenings in the spiritual world and find that in three or four days' time such happenings take place on the physical plane. They will see certain things in etheric pictures and know that tomorrow or in a few days' time this or that will happen.

These faculties of the human soul will be transformed. And what is associated with this? The Being we call the Christ was once on earth in the flesh at the beginning of our era. He will never come again in a physical body, for that was a unique event and will not be repeated. But He will come again in an etheric form in the period indicated. People will learn to perceive Christ inasmuch as through this etheric sight they will grow towards Him. He does not now descend as far as the physical body but only as far as the etheric body; people must therefore grow to the stage where He can be perceived. For Christ spoke truly when He said: 'I am with you always, even unto the end of the days of earth.' He is present in our spiritual world, and those especially blessed can always see Him in this spiritual, etheric world.

A man who was convinced with particular intensity through such perception was Paul—in the vision at Damascus. But this etheric sight will develop in individual human beings as a natural faculty. In days to come it will be more and more possible for people to experience what Paul experienced at Damascus.

We are now able to grasp quite a different aspect of spiritual science. We realize that it is a preparation for the actual event of the new appearance of Christ. Christ will appear again inasmuch as with their etheric sight people will raise themselves to Him. When this is understood, spiritual science is disclosed as the means of preparing people to recognize the return of Christ, in order that it shall not be their misfortune to overlook this event but that they shall be mature enough to grasp the great happening of the Second Coming of Christ. People will become capable of seeing etheric bodies and among them, too, the etheric body of Christ; that is to say, they will grow into a world where Christ will be revealed to their newly awakened faculties.

It will then no longer be necessary to amass all kinds of

documentary evidence to prove the existence of Christ; there will be eyewitnesses of the presence of the Living Christ, people who will know Him in His etheric body. And from this experience they will realize that this is the same Being who at the beginning of our era fulfilled the Mystery of Golgotha, that He is indeed the Christ. Just as Paul at Damascus was convinced at the time 'This is Christ', so there will be people whose experiences in the etheric world will convince them that in very truth Christ lives.

The supreme mystery of the age in which we are living is the Second Coming of Christ—that is its true nature. But the materialistic mind will in a certain sense appropriate this event. What has now been said—that all the data of genuine spiritual knowledge point to this age—will often be proclaimed in the years immediately ahead. But the materialistic mind corrupts everything today, and what will happen is that this kind of thinking will be quite incapable of conceiving that the souls of human beings must advance to the stage of etheric sight and therewith to vision of Christ in the etheric body.

Materialistic thinking will conceive of this event as a descent of Christ in the flesh, as an incarnation in the flesh. A numbers of persons in their boundless arrogance will turn this to their own advantage and announce themselves to people as the reincarnated Christ. The near future may therefore bring false Christs, but anthroposophists should be so fully prepared for the spiritual life that they will not confuse the return of Christ in a spiritual body, perceptible only to higher vision, with a return in a physical body of flesh. This will be one of the most terrible temptations besetting mankind and to lead people past this temptation will be the task of those who learn through spiritual science to rise in the true sense to an understanding of the spirit, who try not to drag spirit down into matter but to ascend into the spiritual world themselves. Thus we may speak of the return of Christ and of the fact that we rise to Christ in the spiritual world through acquiring the faculty of etheric vision.

Christ is ever present, but He is in the spiritual world. We can reach Him when we rise into that world. All anthroposophical teaching should be transformed within us into an indomitable will not to allow this event to pass unnoticed but in the time that remains to us gradually to educate human beings who will be capable of developing these new faculties and therewith *to unite anew with Christ.* Otherwise, before such an opportunity could again arise, humanity would have to wait for long, long ages—indeed, until a new incarnation of the Earth. If this event of the return of Christ were to be overlooked, the vision of Christ in the etheric body would be restricted to those who are willing to fit themselves for such an experience through esoteric training. But the really momentous fact of these faculties being acquired by humanity in general, by all people, of this great event being understood by means of faculties developing naturally in everyone—that would be impossible for long, long ages.

Obviously, therefore, there is something in our age that justifies the existence and the work of spiritual science in the world. Its aim is not merely to satisfy theoretical needs or scientific curiosity. To prepare people for this great event, to prepare them to take their rightful place in the epoch in which they live and with clarity of understanding and knowledge to perceive what is actually present but may pass people by without being brought to fruition—such is the aim of spiritual science.

4. Building for the Future: The Rediscovery of Form

The transformation of consciousness that Rudolf Steiner describes will inevitably be expressed in changed relationships not only to the environment in which we live, but to people around us, and to the greater powers we perceive underlying and guiding evolution.

Architecture today is a major force in all our lives, all too often a source of oppression or even of the violence and alienation of the inner cities. Yet few answers to the urban dilemma can be reached so long as buildings are conceived in the external way that has led to this situation. Rudolf Steiner reached to the deeper sources of our living together with the world as we change it by building homes, towns, work-places, churches, etc. A building does not just arise from external conditions and forces—nor is it something that is, or at any rate need be, imposed by our selfish needs upon the environment. Steiner goes back to the fundamental gestures and collective movements of human beings, to show how these were then externalized and brought to consciousness as artistic creativity. Forms arising from gesture in this way can still allow us to be at one with our world, and also to bring it into the sphere of the moral and spiritually alive that we have seen leads on to the awareness of Christ. A building based on those forms could lead us from 'law' to 'love'; it could even be itself the expression of human freedom, not as a 'statement' from the architect but as a place that freely invites us and opens itself up to the activities for which it was built.

The sculptural-architectural form of the Goetheanum thus makes it more than the centre of the international movement that has grown from Steiner's work. The Second Goetheanum is a place of continuing creativity (as the recent reworking of the interior to include much of Rudolf Steiner's original designs shows). And it is a realization of the way spirituality can become loving transformation of the world. In its 'living concrete' it is indeed building the future.

The basis of all artistic creation is to be found in a state of being or consciousness that existed before the beginnings of recorded history. This was a particular consciousness that was active in human beings at the dawn of historical times, and was a remnant of an old human clairvoyance. This state of being also belongs to the fourth post-Atlantean epoch, the age of ancient Greece and Rome. Although ancient Egyptian culture belongs to the third post-Atlantean epoch, all that was expressed in Egyptian art belongs to the fourth epoch. By the time of the fourth post-Atlantean epoch this consciousness gave rise to inner feeling in a way that made human beings able to perceive how human movement, bearing and gestures developed the human form and figure out of the etheric into the physical.

To understand what I mean, try to imagine that in those times, when there was a true comprehension of artistic will, the actual sight of a flower or tendril was far less important than the feeling: 'I have to carry something heavy, I bend my back and generate with my own form the forces that make me, a human being, shape myself in a way that will enable me to bear this weight.'

Human beings felt within themselves what they had to bring to expression in their own gestures. One movement was used to grip hold of something, while another was an expression of carrying; stretching your hands out in front gives you a feeling that you are carrying something. Out of such gestures arose the lines and shapes leading over into art. Within your own human nature you can sense how the human being can go beyond what eyes see and other senses perceive by becoming a part of the universe as a whole. You take up a position in the universe as a whole when you notice that you cannot just saunter along when carrying something heavy. Out of a feeling for lines of force, which one has to develop inwardly, arises artistic creation. These lines of force are nowhere to be found in external reality.

When engaged in spiritual research one often comes upon a wonderful Akashic picture depicting the joining together of a number of human beings into a whole in an ordered and harmonious way. Imagine a kind of stage surrounded by an amphitheatre filled with spectators. In the centre people are walking round in a procession. This is not supposed to create a naturalistic impression in the spectators but a sense of something lofty or indeed supersensible. Seen from above it would look like this:

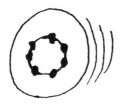

And the side-view would show a group of people walking in a circular procession one behind the other, surrounded by the spectators.

These people portray something of great significance, something that does not exist in the physical world but can only be expressed in analogies. They portray something that brings human beings into connection with the macrocosm. In those times it was a question of representing the relationship of the earthly forces to those of the sun. How can this relationship come to be felt? It is like feeling the carrying of a load. Earthly things rest squarely on the ground, but when they endeavour to wrest themselves free—if you imagine the forces necessary for this—a pointed shape emerges. The human being's state of being bound to the earth is therefore expressed by a shape that has a wide base and runs upwards to a point. Sensing these forces, people felt that they were standing on the earth.

In a similar way they also became aware of their connection with the sun. The sun works downwards towards the earth, and they expressed this by portraying the lines of force raying inwards, just as the sun, in its apparent journey round the earth, sends its rays down towards a mid-point.

These two alternating representations give you the earth motif and the sun motif carried in antiquity by the people who formed the circling procession. Round them sat the spectators, and in the centre the actors passed around in procession, alternately one with the earth motif and one with the sun motif, whose raying-in can also be described as a striving-outwards of sun forces.

Initially this force, this cosmic tension of earth and sun, was felt, and only subsequently did people begin to consider how they might portray it. The best medium for the purposes of artistic expression proved to be a plant or tree whose forms run upwards to a point from a wider base, alternated with palms. Plants having a form like a wide bud were alternated with palms. The palms represented the sun forces, and bud-forms running upwards to a point the earth forces.

People learnt to feel their position within the cosmos and created, so to speak, certain form relationships. Subsequently, on reflection, they selected certain plants as a means of expression, instead of having to create artistic objects for the purpose. The choice of suitable plants was the artistically creative act which was in turn the result of a living experience of cosmic connections. Thus the creative urge in human beings is no mere wish to imitate things in the world around them. The artistic representation of natural things only became a part of art at a later stage. When people no longer realized that palms were used to express the sun forces, they began to think that the ancients had simply imitated palms in their designs. This was never the case; the people of antiquity used the leaves of palms because they typified the sun forces. All true artistic creation has arisen from a superabundance of forces in the nature of the human being—forces that cannot find expression in external life and which strive to do so through our consciousness of our connection with the universe as a whole.

In both science and art, considerations and perceptions have been misled and confused by a certain idea which will be very difficult to erase. It is the idea that complexity must arise from simplicity. This is just not true. For example, the construction of the human eye is much simpler than that in many of the lower animals. The course of evolution is often from the complex to the simple, so that the most intricate interlacing finally resolves into a straight line. In many instances, simplification is the later stage, and we will not acquire a true conception of evolution until we realize this.

What people sensed in those ancient times, and what was presented to the spectators seated round about as a depiction of living, cosmic forces, was later simplified into ornamental lines summarizing what had once been a living experience. The complexity of human evolution honed down into the simple lines of an ornamental border might be drawn like this:

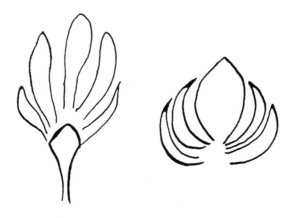

In the alternating patterns you have a simplified reproduction of those people circling in procession with earth motif, sun motif, earth motif, sun motif and so on. What human beings felt and experienced in those ancient times is here summarized in an ornamental border. This decorative motif was already a feature of Mesopotamian art, and it is also found in Greek art as the so-called 'palm motif' either in this form or a similar one resembling the lotus petal.

This alternation of earth and sun motif presented itself to the artistic feeling of people as a really decorative ornamental theme in the truest sense. Later on it was forgotten that in this decorative ornament they were looking at an unconscious reproduction of a very ancient dance gesture, a festive, ceremonial dance. Nonetheless, this fact has thus been preserved in the 'palm motif'...

All this goes to show that in order to understand the forms in the interior of the Goetheanum*—the forms that are to adorn it—we first have to reach an understanding of the artistic principle from which they have arisen. In trying to understand the principle of the interior space formed by our two half domes, or, more correctly, three-quarter domes, we could do worse than imagine how a jelly mould works.

The jelly takes shape inside the mould, and when the mould is upturned and removed the jelly reveals all the forms that are present in negative inside the mould:

The same principle may be applied in the case of the interior design of our building, only here there is no jelly inside but the living word of spiritual science moving and weaving in the form possible for it. All that is enclosed within the spatial shapes, all that is spoken here and done within them, must adapt to them as the jelly adapts to the negative forms of the jelly mould. We should feel the walls as the living negative of the words that are spoken and the deeds

---

* Rudolf Steiner's main architectural work, the original largely a wooden structure (subsequently burned down), the later or Second Goetheanum in sculptural concrete. It is named from the poet and scientist Johann Wolfgang von Goethe, whose ideas of metamorphosis helped inspire its organic, living form. Today the building is the centre and spiritual home of the Anthroposophical Society. On its conception and evolution see Hagen Biesantz and Arne Klingborg, *The Goetheanum* (London 1979) and Rex Raab, Arne Klingborg and Ake Fant, *Eloquent Concrete* (London 1979).

that are done in the building. That is the principle of the
interior design here. Think of the living words of spiritual
science as they come up against these walls, hollowing them
out in accordance with their profundity of meaning. They
hollow out shapes that fit their meaning. This is why these
interior forms are shaped as they are, worked out of the flat
surface.

I at least felt from the outset that it was right to work with
gouge and mallet in such a way that the chisel was struck with
the left hand from the start in the direction in which the
surface is to lie when it is finished. So we strike in this
direction from the start. On other occasions we hold the
gouge at right angles to the surface.

I would have preferred it greatly if a surface like this one
[*pointing to one of the architraves*] could have been avoided.
It will not be right until this round part here has been
removed. It would have been better to work with a gouge
from the start, for then there would have been no bulge but
only a surface. What we must do is feel from the models how
the interior shaping is the garment, the sculpted garment for
the spiritual science that is given to us in this building. Just as
the interior shaping has the quality of being hollowed out
from the inner surface, so will the outer shaping be something
that is laid upon the outside. Inside there must be a sense of
having been hollowed out. Working on the model I was able
to sense this. It was a matter of finding an inner sense for a
shape enclosing a space.

This is why even Adolf Hildebrand's book* leaves one
dissatisfied on this score. He certainly has ideas about the
effects forms can have, but what he lacks is an ability to feel
his way right into the forms themselves. In his opinion they

---

* Adolf von Hildebrand, *Das Problem der Form in der bildenden Kunst*
(The Problem of Form in the Visual Arts) (Strasbourg 1913).

are something you look at with your eyes. Here [*pointing to a form*] you should experience the form within yourself so that, holding the gouge in a particular way, you grow to love the surface you are creating, the surface that is coming into being here under your mallet and gouge. I must confess that I cannot help caressing a surface like this once it has been created. We must grow to love it, so that we live in it with inner feeling instead of thinking of it as something that is merely there for our eyes to look at.

The other day I was told, after a lecture, that some bright spark had complained about the way we attach such importance to details in the physical world, as shown, for example, by the way each of the columns is made from a different wood. This shows how little our work has been understood. Even this very intelligent person cannot understand that the columns have to be made from different woods. He has not paused to consider what answer he would give if he were asked why a violin has different strings. Why not simply use four A-strings? The use of different woods is a reality in precisely the same sense. We could no more use only one kind of wood than we could have only A-strings on a violin. Our concern is with real inner necessities.

One can never do more than mention a few details in these matters. The whole conception of our building, and what must be expressed in it, is based upon immense wisdom, but a wisdom that is at the same time very intimate. The forms in it are obviously nowhere to be found in the physical world. Any apparent resemblance in our building to shapes found in animals or in the human body arises from the fact that higher spirits, who work in nature, create in accordance with the same forces with which we are creating; nature is expressing the very things we are also expressing here in our building. It is not a question of imitating nature but of expressing what exists as pure etheric form. It is like asking how I would imagine myself if I were to leave the external world of sense-perceptions out of account and seek instead surroundings that would express in forms my own inner being.

I am well aware that the sculpted forms of the capitals and the rest of the interior will meet with some criticism. Nevertheless, every single one of these shapes has its own *raison d'être*. Someone working on this column down here [*pointing*] with mallet and gouge will carve more deeply than up here. It would be nonsense to demand symmetry. There must be living progression, not symmetry. Everything about the columns and architraves in the interior is a necessary consequence of having the two cylinders of the building— one smaller, one larger—surmounted by the two intersecting domes. I cannot express this any more precisely than by saying that if the radius of the small dome were any larger or smaller in proportion to the large one, then each of these forms would have to be quite different, just as the little finger of a dwarf is different from that of a giant.

It was not only the differences in dimension, but the differences in the forms themselves that called forth an overwhelming sense of responsibility for making everything just as it is now, down to the smallest detail. Each separate part of a living organism has to exist within, and in accordance with the whole. It would be nonsense to want to change a nose and put another organ in its place. Similarly a big toe as well as a small toe would have to be different if the nose were different. Just as no one in his senses would wish to remodel the nose, so it is impossible that any form here should be other than it is. If one form were changed the whole building would have to be different, for the whole is conceived as a living, organic form.

What was, in the early days of art, a kind of instinctive perception of human gestures transformed into artistic form must now enter with consciousness into the feeling life of human beings. This is the step forward to be taken in our time. In this way we shall have, in our interior designs, etheric forms that are truly alive, and we shall feel how all that is to live in these spaces must make its impression precisely in this way. It simply cannot be otherwise.

Recently I received two letters from a man who used to belong to our anthroposophical movement, though he left it about ten years ago. He wanted to be allowed to design the windows of our building, insisting that he was very well qualified to do so. But when you see the windows you will understand that they could only be made by someone who has followed our work right up to the present. Just as the impression of my hand in clay will not look like an ox's head, so must the true impression of our spiritual science show in our interior design, and so must our spiritual science let in the sunlight through the windows in a way that harmonizes with its own nature. As we have said, the whole building is constructed according to the principle of the jelly mould, only in place of the jelly it is filled with spiritual science and all the sacred things that inspire us. This has always been the case in art, and above all it was so in the days when human beings perceived in their dim, mystical life of feeling the alternation of the principles of earth and sun in the living dance, and then portrayed the dance in the 'palm motif'. So it must be when it is a question of penetrating the sense-perceptible shell of natural and human existence and expressing in forms things that lie behind the realm of sense-perception—if, that is to say, we are fortunate enough to be able to carry this building through. How inner progress is related to onward-flowing evolution will be perceptible in the building, in its proportions, its forms, its designs and paintings.

I wanted to present you with these thoughts so as to help you avoid being misled by modern conceptions of art, which have put all true understanding on one side. A good example of this is the belief that the Corinthian capital is supposed to depict a little basket with acanthus leaves around it. The truth is that something springing from the very depths of human evolution has been expressed in the Corinthian capital. In the same way we shall feel that what surrounds us in our building is the expression of something living in the depths of human nature, behind the experiences and events of the physical plane.

Today I only wanted to speak about this aspect of our building and, in connection with this, about a certain chapter in the history of art.

Other opportunities might present themselves in the coming weeks to speak to you of other things in connection with some of the motifs in the building. I shall seize every available opportunity, and any situation that presents itself, to approach the complex but spiritually natural and necessary foundation on which our building rests.

Nowadays it is not at all easy to speak about artistic questions, for naturalism, the principle of imitation, really dominates the whole realm of art. So far as the artist himself is concerned, naturalism has arisen out of a very simple principle, though for other people it seems to have arisen from something less simple. While he is training, the artist must, of course, imitate the works of his teacher in order to learn something. But people today have an instinctive feeling that they do not want the situation of authority implicit in the pupil-teacher relationship, so in the place of the teacher they put nature, which they imitate instead. It is easy for the artist not to go beyond imitating what he sees in front of him; and for the layman naturalism is a matter of course.

Where on earth can ordinary people find any clues by which to arrive at ideas about forms like those they see in our building? They will tap their forehead and shrug their shoulders, considering themselves lucky if they find anything at all to take hold of, such as some detail that remotely resembles a nose. Although this may be negative, they are delighted to have discovered anything at all. Since all the arts nowadays lack anything that might point to what lies behind nature, lay people are likely to be thankful for anything they can find that resembles something they recognize. This confusion that leads to art being seen as something resembling nature is understandable. But genuine art does not resemble anything at all; it is something in itself, sufficient unto itself. . .

And now, please observe carefully the element of support and weight in the Greek temple. Follow it to the point where it becomes crystallized craftsmanship in Gothic architecture. If we penetrate it with our artistic feeling we realize that the Greek temple is something at rest within itself, at rest within the earthly forces. Fundamentally all the forces of these buildings rest within the earthly. Especially in the Greek temple, wherever you look you will observe the force of gravity in union with the earth. Throughout the Greek temple you can study aspects of gravitational force at work. Its very forms reveal its union with the earth.

Imagine now the fundamental form in our building here, a form that will confront people from outside as they approach. Here is a rough sketch of it:

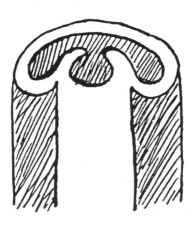

What is essentially characteristic about this design motif? If you compare it with the Greek temple you will discover the difference. The Greek motif is complete in itself. If it is a wall, it is just a vertical wall. Our motif here, on the other hand, is not merely a wall, for it only has meaning if it comes 'alive' and is not just a static wall but allows things to 'grow' out of it. Here the wall is not merely a wall, it is alive, just like a living organism that allows elevations and depressions to grow harmoniously out of itself. The wall has come alive— that is the difference.

However many columns there are in a Greek temple, the whole is none the less governed by gravity. In our building, however, nothing is mere wall. The essential thing is that forms grow out of the wall. When the time comes for us to walk about inside our building we shall find many sculpted forms, a continuous relief joining the capitals, and other forms on plinths and architraves. What is their significance? It is that they grow out of the wall, and the wall is their soil without which they could not exist.

In the interior of our building there will be a great deal of such relief carving in wood; forms which, although they are not to be found elsewhere in the physical world, represent an onward-flowing evolution. Beginning with a few forceful bars between the Saturn columns at the back, there will be a kind of symphonic progression of harmonies culminating in a finale in the east of the building. But these forms are no more present in the outer physical world than are melodies. These forms are walls that have come alive. Physical walls do not come alive, but etheric walls, spiritual walls do indeed come alive.

It would take a long time to explain why the art of sculptural relief only now assumes its true meaning, but I will give you just an indication of what I really have in mind. An eminent contemporary artist has said some clever things about the art of the relief. He explains his conception of it thus: 'To make this quite clear, think of two panes of glass standing parallel to one another with a shape between them.' Seen in section it would look like this; you look through the glass walls in the direction of the arrow and see the shape between them.

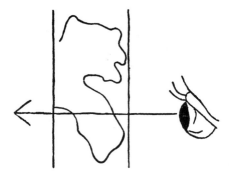

The shape is parallel to the glass walls and touches them at its highest points. 'The shape therefore occupies a space of even depth since its parts are arranged within the limits of this depth. Seen from the front through the pane of glass, on the one hand the shape represents a recognizable two-dimensional picture, and on the other hand an assumption of the amount of space it occupies is made easy even if the shape is complicated. The shape exists within a flat layer of even depth and all its forms spread out within this layer...'

What does all this mean? It means that the author is trying to form a conception of what a relief really is. But he is taking the eye as his starting-point and trying to show that a relief comes about if you imagine it against a back wall made of glass and bounded by another wall of glass in front. Unlike Hildebrand's conception using glass walls, our conception of the relief is of something alive. We want to show how a relief is alive, for it has no meaning if it is simply a shape attached to a wall. It is only meaningful if it gives a sense of the wall itself being alive and giving birth to the shape.

There is a relief in existence which is full of meaning, only we cannot normally see it. It is a relief based on the right concepts: the surface of the wall reveals what it depicts. This relief is the surface of the earth itself, including the plant cover. In order to study it properly, however, we would have to step out into space and look back at its surface from there. The earth is the living surface that brings forth shapes. This is what our relief is to be like, giving us a clear sense that the wall is alive, just as we know that the earth is alive and can bring forth the plant world from its depths. Then we shall have achieved a genuine art of relief. To do more than this would be to sin against the essential nature of the relief. Looking down at the great relief of the earth we see people and animals moving upon it, but they do not belong to the relief. Of course we could include them in the relief, since the arts can be developed in all directions, but in essence it would then no longer be a pure art of relief.

Through the forms in its interior our building must speak in the language of the gods. Think for a moment of human beings living on the actual surface of the earth. We need not even draw on our spiritual science but can simply turn to the legend of Paradise. If human beings had remained in Paradise they would have looked from outside upon the wonderful relief of the earth with its flora. Instead, they were transplanted down to the earth where they now live within the relief without being able to see it from outside. They have departed from Paradise and the speech of the gods cannot reach them because the speech of the earth is louder and drowns it. If we pay heed to the organs of the gods which they themselves created when, as Elohim, they gave the earth to man, if we pay heed to the etheric forms of the plants and mould our walls in accordance with them, then—just as nature created the larynx in human beings in order that they

Rudolf Steiner, First Goetheanum (Dornach, Switzerland). The highly carved wooden exterior of the building, and the rich artistic elaboration of the interior of the interlocking domes were alike destroyed by fire; but Rudolf Steiner's motifs and pictorial designs have recently been incorporated under the direction of Christian Hitsch into the interior of the present-day, sculptured concrete Goetheanum building (Dornach).

might speak—we are indeed creating larynxes through which the gods may speak to us. When we listen attentively to the forms in our walls which are larynxes for the gods, we are seeking the way back to Paradise.

I will speak about painting in another lecture, but today I want to dwell on the special kind of relief and sculpture to which the building we are inaugurating today is to be initially devoted. We have endeavoured to gain a sense of how a relief may become an organ of speech for the gods, and on some future occasion we will speak of how colours must become soul organs for the gods. Our age has very little understanding for the kind of conceptions that must inspire us if we are really to fulfil our task in the creation of our Goetheanum building.

We have seen how the Greek temple was the dwelling place of the god, and the Christian church the enclosure around the congregation seeking union with their god. What, then, is our building to be? Its fundamental character is revealed even in its ground plan and in its domed shape.

It has two sections, and the architectural forms of both are equally important, unlike the Christian church, where a difference is made between the chancel for the altar and the nave for the congregation. The difference in size simply signifies that in the large cupola the physical aspect is paramount, while in the smaller one we have tried to make the spiritual aspect predominant. The very form expresses aspiration to the spirit. Every single detail must express this aspiration to the spirit, inasmuch as we are striving to create an organ for the speech of the gods.

I have said that those who really understand our building fully will set aside lying and wrongdoing, and that the building can become a 'lawgiver'. The truth of this can be studied in the individual forms. In a number of places in the architraves and the other forms you will find this specific feature [*begins drawing*]. Nowhere is it without meaning. Just as no part of the larynx is without meaning and no words would emerge if the larynx did not have the right form in the right place, so if you make a hollow shape here in the building, with a projection above it resembling eaves, this is an exact expression of the fact that this building must be filled with the feelings of those whose hearts stream together in love.

Nothing in this architecture is there for its own sake alone. One form leads over into another; or, if the forms have a threefold character, the middle part is the bridge between the other two. Here, in rough, are the forms of doors and windows:

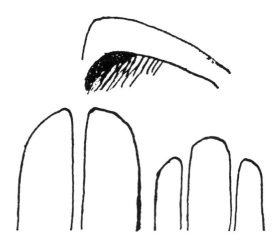

Whereas forms in sculpture live in three dimensions, the relief is an overcoming of the two-dimensional surface so that it can begin to include the third dimension. We do not discover this by merely taking the viewpoint of an observer or spectator; we realize it when we gain a living sense of how the earth allows the plants to grow out of itself.

5. Educating for the Future: Love and Knowledge in the Waldorf School

There are now Waldorf Schools in so many countries of the world, from Israel to Peru, from Scandinavia to South Africa, that it would be tedious as well as unnecessary to trace their family tree back to the original school in Stuttgart, where the movement began. A Waldorf School in their town or city is a familiar sight to many.

The aim of the schools is in no way to teach the children Rudolf Steiner's ideas—that will be a personal exploration they will undertake, if they wish to, freely and at the time they feel the need. The foundation of the educational movement he started is not to be found in the communication of ideas at all, as he makes clear in the extract that follows. It lies in our love of the children who come to be educated, and in the spiritual reality of the human relationships of which they form from the beginning an active part. Steiner's method of deriving values, deriving meaning, from a deepened relationship to the subject itself put him ahead of virtually all contemporary thinkers in his reform of the curriculum and a developmental approach that bases itself on the child. As educators everywhere have to face the increasingly rapid changes in ideas and technology which make a nonsense of the simultaneously imposed rigidities of the curriculum, the recognition accorded an educational approach that brings out the inner freedom and mobility of the child and an imaginative ability to look at things in different ways is no longer limited to those discontented with the mainstream. Here more than anywhere else we can see the results of the universalism of Rudolf Steiner's approach, his vision—revealed not only to those who want to study his work,

but in the qualities that will be needed for the new world-era on
which we are all in whatever different ways now embarking.

What sort of person must one be today if one wishes to pursue some calling based on knowledge—for instance on the knowledge of man? One must be objective! This is to be heard all over the place today, in every hole and corner. Of course one must be objective, but the question is whether or not this objectivity is based on a lack of paying due heed to what is essential in any particular situation.

Now for the most part people have the idea that love is far more subjective than anything else in life, and that it would be utterly impossible for anyone who loves to be objective. For this reason when knowledge is spoken about today love is never mentioned seriously. True, it is deemed fitting, when a young man is applying himself to acquire knowledge, to exhort him to do so with love, but this mostly happens when the whole way in which knowledge is presented is not at all likely to develop love in anybody. But the essence of love, the giving of oneself to the world and its phenomena, is in any case not regarded as knowledge. Nevertheless for real life love is the greatest power of knowledge. And without this love it is utterly impossible to attain to a knowledge of man which could form the basis of a true art of education. Let us try to picture this love, and see how it can work in the special sphere of an education founded on a knowledge of man drawn from spiritual science, from anthroposophy.

The child is entrusted to us to be educated, to be taught. If our thinking in regard to education is founded on anthroposophy we do not represent the child to ourselves as something we must help to develop so that he approaches nearer and nearer to some social human ideal, or whatever it may be. For this human ideal can be completely abstract. And today such a human ideal has already become something which can assume as many forms as there are political, social and other parties. Human ideals change according to whether one swears by liberalism, conservatism, or by some other programme, and so the child is led slowly in some particular direction in order to become what is held to be right for mankind. This is carried to extreme lengths in present-day Russia [1924]. Generally speaking, however, it is more or less how people think today, though perhaps somewhat less radically.

This is no starting-point for the teacher who wants to educate and teach on the basis of anthroposophy. He does not make an 'idol' of his opinions. For an abstract picture of man, towards which the child shall be led, is an idol, it is in no sense a reality. The only reality which could exist in this field would be at most if the teacher were to consider himself as an ideal and were to say that every child must become like him. Then one would at least have touched on some sort of reality, but the absurdity of saying such a thing would at once be obvious.

What we really have before us in this young child is a being who has not yet begun his physical existence, but has brought down his spirit and soul from pre-earthly worlds, and has plunged into a physical body bestowed on him by parents and ancestors. We look upon this child as he lies there before us in the first days of his life with indeterminate features and with unorganized, undirected movements. We follow day by day, week by week how the features grow more and more defined, and become the expression of what is working to the surface from the inner life of soul. We observe further how the whole life and movements of the child become more consequent and directed, how something of the nature of spirit and soul is working its way to the surface from the inmost depths of his being. Then, filled with holy awe and reverence, we ask: 'What is it that is here working its way to

the surface?' And so with heart and mind we are led back to
the human being himself, when as soul and spirit he dwelt in
the soul-spiritual pre-earthly world from which he has
descended into the physical world, and we say: 'Little child,
now that you have entered through birth into earthly
existence you are among human beings, but previously you
were among spiritual, divine beings.' What once lived among
spiritual-divine beings has descended in order to live among
human beings. We see the divine made manifest in the child.
We feel as though standing before an altar. There is however
one difference. In religious communities it is customary for
human beings to bring their sacrificial offerings to the altars,
so that these offerings may ascend into the spiritual world;
now we feel ourselves standing as it were before an altar
turned the other way; now the gods allow their grace to
stream down in the form of divine-spiritual beings, so that
these beings, acting as messengers of the gods, may unfold
what is essentially human on the altar of physical life. We
behold in every child the unfolding of cosmic laws of a divine-
spiritual nature; we see how God creates in the world. In its
highest, most significant form this is revealed in the child.
Hence every single child becomes for us a sacred riddle, for
every single child embodies this great question—not 'How is
he to be educated so that he approaches some "idol" which
has been thought out?' but 'How shall we foster what the
gods have sent down to us into the earthly world?' We learn
to know ourselves as helpers of the divine-spiritual world,
and above all we learn to ask: 'What may be the result if we
approach education with this attitude of mind?'

Education in the true sense proceeds out of just such an
attitude. What matters is that we should develop our education and teaching on the basis of such thoughts as these.
Knowledge of man can only be won if love for mankind—in
this case love for the child—becomes the mainspring of our

work. If this is so, then the teacher's calling becomes a priestly calling, for then the educator becomes the steward of what is the will of the gods to carry out with man.

Here again it might appear as though something obvious is being said in rather different words. But it is not so. As a matter of fact, in today's unsocial world order, which only wears an outer semblance of being social, the very opposite occurs. Educationists pursue an 'idol' for mankind, not seeing themselves as nurturers of something they must first learn to know when actually face to face with the child.

An attitude of mind such as I have described cannot work in an abstract way, it must work spiritually, while always keeping the practical in view. Such an attitude, however, can never be acquired by accepting theories quite unrelated and alien to life; it can only be gained if one has a feeling, a sense for every expression of life, and can enter with love into all its manifestations.

Today there is a great deal of talk about educational reform. Since the War there has been talk of a revolution in education. We have experienced this. Every possible approach to a new education is thought out, and pretty well everybody is concerned in some way or other with how this reform is to be brought about. Either one approaches some institution about to be founded with one's proposals or at the very least one suggests this or that as one's idea of how education should take shape. And so it goes on. There is a great deal of talk about methods of education; but do you see what kind of impression all this makes when one surveys, quite without prejudice, what the various societies for the reform of education, down to the most radical, put forward today in their educational programmes? I do not know whether many people take into account what kind of impression is made when one is faced with so many pro-grammes issuing from associations and societies for educational reform. One gets the impression: Good heavens, how clever people are today! For indeed everything which comes about like this is frightfully clever. I do not mean this ironically, but quite seriously. There has never been a time when there was so much cleverness as there is in our era.

There we have it, all set out. *Paragraph 1.* How shall we educate so that the forces of the child may be developed naturally? *Paragraph 2 ... Paragraph 3 ...* and so on. People today of any profession or occupation, and of any social class can sit down together and work out such programmes; everything we get in this way in paragraphs 1 to 30 will be delightfully clever, for today one knows just how to formulate everything theoretically. People have never been so skilful in formulating things as they are today. Then such a programme, a number of programmes can be submitted to a committee or to Parliament. This again is very clever. Now something may perhaps be deleted or added according to party opinion, and something extremely clever emerges, even if at times strongly coloured by 'party'. Nothing can be done with it, however, for all this is quite beside the point.

Waldorf School education never started off with such a programme.* I have no wish to boast, but naturally, had this been our purpose, we could also have produced some kind of programme no less clever than those of many an association for educational reform. The fact that we should have to reckon with reality might perhaps prove a hindrance and then the result would be more stupid. With us however there was never any question of a programme. From the outset we were never interested in principles of educational method which might later on be somehow incorporated in a legalized

---

* The first Waldorf School was founded under Rudolf Steiner's guidance in 1919 in Stuttgart. See further in Christopher Clouder and Martyn Rawson, *Waldorf Education* (Edinburgh 1998).

Harduf Waldorf School, near Nazareth, Israel.

Photo: Brien Masters

Edinburgh Rudolf Steiner School kindergarten, Scotland.

Photo: Aliki Sapountzi

educational system. What did interest us was reality, absolute true reality. What was this reality? To begin with here were children, a number of child-individualities with varying characteristics. One had to learn what these were, one had to get to know what was inherent in these children, what they had brought down with them, what was expressed through their physical bodies. First and foremost then there were the children. And then there were teachers. You can stand up as strongly as you like for the principle that the child must be educated in accordance with his individuality—that stands in all the programmes of reform—but nothing whatever will come of it. For on the other hand, besides the children, there are a number of teachers, and the point is to know what these teachers can accomplish in relation to these children. The school must be run in such a way that one does not set up an abstract ideal, but allows the school to develop out of the teachers and out of the pupils. And these teachers and pupils are not present in an abstract kind of way, but are quite concrete, individual human beings. That is the gist of the matter. Then we are led by virtue of necessity to build up a true education based on a real knowledge of man. We cease to be theoretical and become practical in every detail.

Waldorf School education, the first manifestation of an education based on anthroposophy, is actually the practice of education as an art, and is therefore able to give only indications of what can be done in this or that case. We have no great interest in general theories, but so much the greater is our interest in impulses coming from anthroposophy which can give us a true knowledge of man, beginning, as here of course it must do, with the child. But today our crude observation completely ignores what is most characteristic in the progressive stages of life. I would say that some measure of inspiration must be drawn from spiritual science if today we are to develop a right sense for what should be brought to the child. At the present time people know extraordinarily little about man and mankind. They imagine that our present state of existence is the same as it was in the fourteenth, fifteenth and sixteenth centuries, and indeed as it has always been. They picture the ancient Greeks and the ancient Egyptians as being very similar to the man of today. And if we go back still further, according to the views of present-day natural science, history becomes enveloped in mist until those beings emerge which are half ape, half man. No interest is taken, however, in penetrating into the great differences that exist between the historical and prehistorical epochs of mankind.

Let us study the human being as he appears to us today, beginning with the child up to the change of teeth. We see quite clearly that his physical development runs parallel with his development of soul and spirit. Everything that manifests as soul and spirit has its exact counterpart in the physical—both appear together, both develop out of the child together. Then, when the child has come through the change of teeth, we see how the soul is already freeing itself from the body. On the one side we shall be able to follow a development of soul and spirit in the child, and on the other side his physical development. The two sides however are not as yet clearly separated. If we continue to follow the development further into the time between puberty and about the 21st year the separation becomes much more defined, and then when we come to the 27th or 28th year—speaking now of present-day humanity—nothing more can be seen of the way in which the soul-spiritual is connected with the physical body. What a person does at this age can be perceived on the one hand in the soul-spiritual life and on the other hand in the physical life, but the two cannot be brought into any sort of connection. At the end of the twenties, man in his soul and spirit has separated himself completely from what is physical, and so it goes on up to the end of his life.

Yet it was not always so. One only believes it to have been so. Spiritual science, studied anthroposophically, shows us clearly and distinctly that what we see in the child today, at the present stage of human evolution, namely, that in his being of soul and spirit the child is completely dependent on his physical-bodily nature and his physical-bodily nature is completely dependent on his being of soul and spirit, this condition persisted right on into extreme old age—a fact that has simply not been noticed. If we go very far back into those times which gave rise to the conception of the patriarchs and ask ourselves what kind of a man such a patriarch really was, the answer must be somewhat as follows. Such a man, in growing old, changed in respect of his bodily nature, but right into extreme old age he continued to feel as only quite young people can feel today. Even in old age he felt his being of soul and spirit to be dependent on his physical body.

Today we no longer feel our physical body to be dependent upon what we think and feel. A dependence of this kind was however felt in the more ancient epochs of civilization. But people also felt after a certain age of life that their bones became harder and their muscles contained certain foreign substances which brought about a sclerotic condition. They felt the waning of their life forces, but they also felt with this physical decline an increase of spiritual forces, actually brought about by the breaking up of the physical. 'The soul is becoming free from the physical body.' So they said when this process of physical decline began. At the age of the patriarchs, when the body was already breaking up, the soul was most able to wrest itself free from the body, so that it was no longer within it. This is why people looked up to the patriarchs with such devotion and reverence, saying: 'Oh, how will it be with me one day, when I am so old? For in old age one can know things, understand things, penetrate into the heart of things in a way that I cannot do now, because I am still building up my physical body.' At that time man could still look into a world order that was both physical and spiritual. This however was in a very remote past. Then came a time when man felt this interdependence of the physical and the soul-spiritual only until about the 50th year. The Greek age followed. What gives the Greek epoch its special value rests on the fact that the Greeks were still able to feel the harmony between the soul-spiritual and the physical-bodily. The Greeks still felt this harmony until the 30th or 40th year. They still experienced in the circulation of the blood what brought the soul into a unity with the physical. The wonderful culture and art of the Greeks was founded on this unity, which transformed everything theoretical into art, and at the same time instilled art with wisdom.

In those times the sculptor worked in such a way that he needed no model, for in his own organization he was aware of the forces permeating the arm or the leg, giving them their form. This was learned, for instance, in the festival games; but today when such games are imitated they have no meaning whatsoever.

If however we have such a sense for the development of mankind then we know what has actually taken place in human evolution. We know too that today we only have a parallelism between the physical-bodily and soul-spiritual until about the 27th or 28th year, to give a quite exact description. (Most people observe this parallelism only up to the age of puberty.) And so we know how the divine-spiritual springs up and grows out of the developing human being. Then we feel the necessary reverence for our task of developing what comes to meet us in the child, that is to say, of developing what is *given* to us and not developing those abstract ideas that have been thought out.

Thus our thoughts are directed to a knowledge of man based on what is individual in the soul. And if we have absorbed such universal, great historical aspects, we shall also be able to approach every educational task in an appropriate manner. Then quite another life will be brought into the class when the teacher enters it, for he will carry the world into it, the physical world and the world of soul and spirit. Then he will be surrounded by an atmosphere of reality, of a real and actual conception of the world, not one which is merely thought out and intellectual. Then he will be surrounded by a world imbued with feeling. Now if we consider what has just been put forward we shall realize a remarkable fact. We shall see that we are founding an education which, by degrees, will come to represent in many respects the very opposite of the characteristic impulse in education at the present time. All manner of humorists with some aptitude for caricature often choose the so-called 'schoolmaster' as an object which can serve their purpose well and on whom they can let loose their derision. Well, if a schoolmaster is endowed with the necessary humour he can turn the tables on those who have caricatured him before the world. But the real point is something altogether different; for if the teacher, versed in present-day educational methods, carries these into school with him, and has therefore no means of learning to know the child, while nevertheless having to deal with the child, how can he be anything other than a stranger to the world? With the school system as it is today, he cannot become anything else; he is torn right out of the world. So we are faced with a truly remarkable situation. Teachers who are strangers to the world are expected to train human beings so that they may get on and prosper in the world.

Let us imagine however that the things about which we have been speaking today become an accepted point of view. Then the relation of the teacher to the children is such that in each individual child a whole world is revealed to him, and not only a human world but a divine-spiritual world manifested on earth. In other words the teacher perceives as many aspects of the world as he has children in his charge. Through every child he looks into the wide world. His education becomes art. It is imbued with the consciousness that what is done has a direct effect on the evolution of the world. Teaching in the sense meant here leads the teacher, in his task of educating, of developing human beings, to a lofty conception of the world. Such a teacher is one who becomes able to play a leading part in the great questions that face civilization. The pupil will never outgrow such a teacher, as is so often the case today. The following situation may arise in a school. Let us suppose that the teacher has to educate according to some idea, some picture of man which he can set before himself. Let us think that he might have 30 children in his class, and among these, led by destiny, were two who, in their inborn capacity, were far more gifted than the teacher himself. What would he want to do in such a case? He would want to form them in accordance with his educational ideal; nothing else would be possible. But how does this work out? Reality does not permit it, and the pupils then outgrow their teacher.

If on the other hand we educate in accordance with reality, if we foster all that manifests in the child as qualities of soul and spirit, we are in the same situation as the gardener is in relation to his plants. Do you think that the gardener knows all these secrets of the plants which he tends? Oh, these plants contain many, many more secrets than the gardener understands; but he can tend them, and perhaps succeed best in caring for those which he does not yet know. His knowledge rests on practical experience; he has 'green fingers'. In the same way it is possible for a teacher who practises an art of education based on reality to stand as educator before children who have genius, even though he himself is certainly no genius. For he knows that he has not to lead his pupils towards some abstract ideal, but that in the child the divine is working in man, is working right through his physical-bodily nature. If the teacher has this attitude of mind he can actually achieve what has just been said. He achieves it by an outpouring love which permeates his work as educator. It is his attitude of mind which is so essential.

6. Working with the Future

The unfolding of higher consciousness, to be reached through human evolution in the future, is the key to what those times will be able to achieve. In a quite modest and hard-working way, it is our task to develop those faculties now which will be the common possession of humanity in times to come. Instead of the platitude that every age is an age of transition, Rudolf Steiner offers us the insight that we are already, if we undertake consciously and freely our own higher development, working with the future.

Ahead of us still lies the 'sixth epoch' of culture—a renewal of civilization in changed form. But we can be creating it now, in two ways. Firstly, we can be bringing together the work and insights of those who already possess the moral and spiritual perception on which that epoch will depend. We can be realizing it even in the way we run groups for study, schools for our children, or banks, farms or businesses. Secondly, we can learn how to recognize from the understanding of the rhythmic epochs of renewal where the signs of the future cultural epoch are already to be found. In the Book of Revelation, or Apocalypse, these rhythmic phases are called the seven primal 'churches' (the word really means 'communities'). The sixth, or for us the-next-to-come, is Philadelphia (which means 'brotherly-and-sisterly love'). Although it does not exist yet outwardly on the earth, for Steiner the roots of it were there to be found— not outwardly, but in a quality of consciousness, one he recognized among the Slavic peoples and their spiritual traditions.

Many characteristics of the sixth epoch of culture will be entirely different from those of our age. Three characteristic traits can be mentioned, of which we must realize that they should be carried in our hearts for the sixth epoch of culture and that it is our task to prepare them for this sixth epoch.

There is lacking in human society nowadays a quality that, in the sixth epoch, will be a characteristic of those people who reach the goal of that epoch, and have not fallen short of it. It is a quality that will not, of course, be found among those who in the sixth epoch have still remained at the stage of savages or barbarians. One of the most significant characteristics of people living on the earth at the peak of culture in the sixth epoch will be a certain moral quality. Little of this quality is perceptible in modern humanity. A person today must be delicately organized for his soul to feel pain when he sees other human beings in the world in less happy circumstances than his own. It is true that more delicately organized natures feel pain at the suffering that is so widespread in the world, but this can only be said of the people who are particularly sensitive. In the sixth epoch, the most highly cultured will not only feel pain such as is caused today by the sight of poverty, suffering and misery in the world, but such individuals will experience the suffering of another human being as their own suffering. If they see a hungry person they will feel the hunger right down into the physical, so acutely indeed that the hunger of the other person will be unendurable to them. The moral characteristic indicated here is that, unlike conditions in the fifth epoch, in the sixth epoch the well-being of the individual will depend entirely upon the well-being of the whole. Just as nowadays the well-being of a single human limb depends upon the health of the whole body, and when the whole body is not healthy the single limb is not up to doing its work, so in the sixth epoch a common consciousness will lay hold of the then civilized humanity and, in a far higher degree than a limb feels the health of the whole body, the individual will feel the suffering, the need, the poverty or the wealth of the whole.

This is the first pre-eminently moral trait that will characterize the cultured humanity of the sixth epoch.

A second fundamental characteristic will be that everything we call the fruits of belief today will depend to a far, far higher degree than is the case today upon the single individuality. Spiritual science expresses this by saying that in every sphere of religion in the sixth epoch complete freedom of thought and a longing for it will so lay hold of people that what a person likes to believe, what religious convictions he holds, will rest wholly within the power of his own individuality. Collective beliefs that exist in so many forms today among the various communities will no longer influence those who constitute the civilized portion of humanity in the sixth epoch of culture. Everyone will feel that complete freedom of thought in the domain of religion is a fundamental right of the human being.

The third characteristic will be that people in the sixth epoch will only be considered to have real knowledge when they recognize the spiritual, when they know that the spiritual pervades the world and that human souls must unite with the spiritual. What is known as science today with its materialistic trend will certainly not be honoured by the name of science in the sixth post-Atlantean epoch. It will be regarded as antiquated superstition, able to pass muster only among those who have remained behind at the stage of the superseded fifth post-Atlantean epoch. Today we regard it as superstition when, let us say, a savage holds the view that no limb ought to be separated from his body at death because this would make it impossible for him to enter the spiritual world as a whole man. Such a man still connects the idea of immortality with pure materialism, with the belief that an impress of his whole form must pass into the spiritual world. He thinks materialistically but believes in immortality. We, today, knowing from spiritual science that the spiritual has to be separated from the body and that only the spiritual passes into the supersensible world, regard such materialistic beliefs in immortality as superstition. Similarly, in the sixth epoch all materialistic beliefs including science, too, will be regarded as antiquated superstition. People as a matter of course will accept as science only such forms of knowledge as are based upon the spiritual, upon pneumatology.

The whole purpose of spiritual science is to prepare in this sense for the sixth epoch of culture. We try to cultivate spiritual science in order to overcome materialism, to prepare the kind of science that must exist in that epoch. We found communities of human beings within which there must be no dogmatic beliefs or any tendency to accept teaching simply because it emanates from one person or another. We found communities of human beings in which everything, without exception, must be built upon the soul's free assent to the teachings. Herein we prepare what spiritual science calls freedom of thought. By coming together in friendly associations for the purpose of cultivating spiritual science, we prepare the culture, the civilization of the sixth post-Atlantean epoch.

But we must look still more deeply into the course of human evolution if we are fully to understand the real tasks of our association and groups. In the first post-Atlantean epoch, too, in communities that in those days were connected with the Mysteries, people cultivated what subsequently prevailed in the second epoch. In the associations peculiar to the first, the ancient Indian epoch, people were concerned with the cultivation of the astral body, which was to be the specific outer task of the second epoch. It would lead much too far today to describe what, in contrast to the external culture of the time, was developed in these associations peculiar to ancient India in order to prepare for the second, ancient Persian epoch. But this may be said that when those people of the ancient Indian epoch came together in order to prepare what was necessary for the second epoch, they felt: 'We have not yet attained, nor have we in us, what we shall have when our souls are incarnated in the next epoch. It still hovers above us.' It was in truth so. In the first epoch of culture, what was to descend from the heavens to the earth in the second epoch still hovered over the souls of human beings. The work achieved on earth by people in intimate assemblies connected with the Mysteries was of such a nature that forces flowed upwards to the spirits of the Higher Hierarchies, enabling them to nourish and cultivate what was to stream down into the souls of human beings as substance and content of the astral body in the second, ancient Persian epoch. The forces that descended at a later stage of maturity into the souls incarnated in the bodies of ancient Persian civilizations were like little children in the first epoch. Forces streaming upwards from the work of human beings below in preparation for the next epoch were received and nurtured by the spiritual world above. So it must be in every epoch of culture.

In our epoch it is the consciousness (or spiritual) soul* that has developed in us through our ordinary civilization and culture. Beginning with the fourteenth, fifteenth and sixteenth centuries, science and materialistic consciousness have laid hold of the human being. This will gradually become more widespread, until by the end of the fifth epoch

---

* The age of the 'consciousness soul' covers the period from 1413 AD, and will continue to around 3575 AD when the sixth epoch is commencing, which will be based upon the development of the 'spirit-self'.

The consciousness soul is the stage of humanity's evolution where consciousness becomes highly individualized, detached, reflexive: it has furthered the emergence of scientific and abstract thought, and, on the other hand, the inner freedom which enables us to rediscover the spirit for ourselves. The spirit-self is the first of the higher clairvoyant members which will be evolved by humanity.

its development will have been completed. In the sixth epoch, however, it is the 'spirit-self' that must be developed within the souls of human beings, just as now the consciousness soul is being developed. The nature of spirit-self is that it must presuppose the existence in human souls of the three characteristics of which I have spoken: social life in which brotherliness prevails, freedom of thought, and pneumatology. These three characteristics are essential in a community of human beings within which the spirit-self is to develop as the consciousness soul develops in the souls of the fifth epoch. We may therefore picture to ourselves that by uniting in brotherliness in working groups something hovers invisibly over our work, something that is like the child of the forces of the spirit-self—the spirit-self that is nurtured by the beings of the Higher Hierarchies in order that it may stream down into our souls when they are again on earth in the sixth epoch of civilization. In our groups we perform work that streams upwards to those forces that are being prepared for the spirit-self.

So you see, it is only through the wisdom of spiritual science itself that we can understand what we are really doing in respect of our connection with the spiritual worlds when we come together in these working groups. The thought that we do this work not only for the sake of our own egos but in order that it may stream upwards into the spiritual worlds, the thought that this work is connected with the spiritual worlds, this is the true consecration of a working group. To cherish such a thought is to permeate ourselves with the consciousness of the consecration that is the foundation of a working group within the Movement. It is therefore of great importance to grasp this fact in its true spiritual sense. We find ourselves together in working groups which, besides cultivating spiritual science, are based on freedom of thought. They will have nothing to do with dogma or coercion of belief, and their work should be of the nature of co-operation among brothers. What matters most of all is to become conscious of the true meaning of the idea of community, saying to ourselves: 'Apart from the fact that as modern souls we belong to the fifth post-Atlantean epoch of culture and develop as individuals, raising individual life more and more out of community life, we must in turn become conscious of a higher form of community, founded in the freedom of love among brothers, as a breath of magic that we breathe in our working groups.'

The deep significance of Western European culture lies in the fact that the quest of the fifth post-Atlantean epoch is the consciousness soul. The task of Western European culture, and particularly of Central European culture, is that people shall develop an individual culture, individual consciousness. This is the task of the present age. Compare this epoch of ours with that of Greece and Rome. The Greek epoch exhibits in a particularly striking form, especially among the civilized Greeks, a consciousness of living within a group soul. A man who was born and lived in Athens felt himself to be first and foremost an 'Athenian'. His community between city and what belonged to the city meant something different to the individual from what community between human beings means today. In our time the individual strives to grow out of and beyond the community, and this is right in the fifth post-Atlantean epoch. In Rome, the human being was first and foremost a Roman citizen, nothing else. But in the fifth epoch we strive above all else to be human in our innermost being, man and nothing else. It is a painful experience in our day to see people fighting against one another on the earth, but this, after all, is just a reaction to the perpetual striving of the fifth epoch for free development of the 'universal human'. Because the different countries and peoples shut themselves off today from one another in hostility, it is all the more necessary to develop, as resistance to this, the force that allows human beings to be human in the full sense, allowing the individual to grow out of and beyond every kind of community. But on the other hand the human being must, in full consciousness, make preparation for communities into which he will enter entirely of his own free will in the sixth epoch. There hovers before us, as a high ideal, a form of community that will so encompass the sixth epoch of culture that civilized human beings will quite naturally meet each other as brothers and sisters.

From many lectures given in past years, we know that Eastern Europe is inhabited by a people whose particular mission it will be in the sixth epoch, and not until the sixth epoch, to bring to definite expression the elementary forces that now lie within them. We know that the Russian peoples will not be ready until the sixth epoch of culture to unfold the forces now within them in an elementary form. The mission of Western and Central Europe is to introduce into mankind qualities that can be introduced by the consciousness soul. This is not the mission of Eastern Europe. Eastern Europe will have to wait until the spirit-self comes down to the earth and can permeate the souls of human beings. This must be understood in the right sense. Understood in the wrong sense it may easily lead to pride and superciliousness, precisely in the East. The height of post-Atlantean culture is reached in the fifth epoch. What will follow in the sixth and seventh epochs will be a descending line of evolution. Nevertheless, this descending evolution in the sixth epoch will be inspired, permeated by the spirit-self. Today the person of Eastern Europe feels instinctively, but often with a perverted instinct, that this is so; only his consciousness of it is, for the most part, extremely hazy and confused. The frequent occurrence of the term 'the Russian man' is quite characteristic. Genius expresses itself in language when instead of saying as we do in the West 'the British, the French, the Italian, the German', Eastern Europe says 'the Russian man'. Many of the Russian intelligentsia attach importance to the use of the expression 'the Russian man'. This is connected deeply with the genius of the particular culture. The term refers to the element of manhood, of brotherhood that is spread over a community. An attempt is made to indicate this by including a word that brings out the 'manhood' in the term. But it is also obvious that the height to be reached in a distant future has not yet been attained, inasmuch as the term includes a word that glaringly contradicts the noun. In the expression 'the Russian man', the adjective really nullifies what is expressed in the noun. For when true manhood is attained there should be no adjective to suggest any element of exclusiveness.

But at a much, much deeper level there lies in members of the Russian intelligentsia the realization that a conception of community, of brotherhood must prevail in times still to come. The Russian soul feels that the spirit-self is to descend, but that it can only descend into a community of people permeated with the consciousness of brotherhood, that it can never spread over a community where there is no consciousness of brotherhood. That is why the Russian intellectuals, as they call themselves, make the following reproach to Western and Central Europe. They say, 'You pay no heed at all to a life of true community. You cultivate only individualism. Everyone wants to be a person on his own, to be an individual only. You drive the personal element, through which every single person feels himself an individuality, to its highest extreme.' This is what echoes across from the East to Western and Central Europe in many reproaches of barbarism and the like. Those who try to realize how things really are accuse Western and Central Europe of having lost all feeling for human connections. Confusing present and future as they do now, these people say, 'It is only in Russia that there is a true and genuine community of life among human beings, a life where everyone feels himself the brother of the other, as the "Little Father" or the "Little Mother" of the other.' The Russian intelligentsia say that the Christianity of Western Europe has not succeeded in developing the essence of human community, but that the Russian still knows what community is.

Alexander Herzen, an excellent thinker who lived in the nineteenth century and belonged to the Russian intellectuals, brought this to its ultimate conclusion by saying, 'In Western Europe there can never be happiness.' No matter what attempts are made, happiness will never come to Western European civilization. There humanity will never find contentment. Only chaos can prevail there. The one and only salvation lies in the Russian nature and in the Russian form of life where people have not yet separated themselves from community, where in their village communities there is still something of the nature of the group soul to which they hold fast. What we call the group soul, out of which mankind has gradually emerged and in which the animal kingdom still lives, that is what is revered by the Russian intelligentsia as something great and significant among their people. They cannot rise to the thought that the community of the future must hover as a high ideal, an ideal that has yet to be realized. They adhere firmly to the thought: 'We are the last people in Europe to retain this life in the group soul. The others have risen out of it; we have retained and must retain it for ourselves.'

Yes, but this life in the group soul does not in reality belong to the future at all, for it is the old form of group soul existence. If it continued it would be a luciferic group soul, a form of life that has remained at an earlier stage, whereas the form of group soul life that is true and must be striven for is what we try to find in spiritual science. But be that as it may, the

urge and the longing of the Russian intellectuals show how
the spirit of community is needed to bring about the descent
of spirit-self. Just as it is being striven for there along a false
path, so must it be striven for in spiritual science along the
true path. What we should like to say to the East is this: 'It is
our task to overcome entirely just what you are trying to
preserve in an external form, namely, an old luciferic-ahri-
manic form of community. In a community of a luciferic-
ahrimanic character there will be coercion of belief as rigid as
that established by the Orthodox Catholic Church in Russia.
Such community will not understand true freedom of
thought; least of all will it be able to rise to the level where
complete individuality is associated with a social life in which
brotherhood prevails. That other form of community would
like to preserve what has remained in blood brotherhood, in
brotherhood purely through the blood. Community that is
founded not upon the blood, but upon the spirit, upon
community of souls, is what must be striven for along the
paths of spiritual science. We must try to create communities
in which the factor of blood no longer has a voice. Naturally,
the factor of blood will continue, it will live itself out in family
relationships, for what must remain will not be eradicated.
But something *new* must arise! What is significant in the child
will be retained in the forces of old age, but in his later years
the human being must receive new forces.'

The factor of blood is not meant to encompass great
communities of human beings in the future. That is the error
that is filtering from the East into the dreadful events of
today. A war has blazed up under the heading of community
of blood among the Slavic peoples. Into these fateful times all
those elements are entering of which we have just heard,
elements that in reality have in them the right kernel, namely,
the instinctive feeling that the spirit-self can only manifest in
a community where brotherhood prevails. It must not, how-

After Rudolf Steiner, designs for the cupola of the Goetheanum showing the cultural epochs of humanity: here we see the Blue Angel with the representatives of Slavic humanity and the culture whose spiritual qualities are the basis of evolution in the coming Sixth Epoch.

ever, be a community of blood; it must be a community of souls. What grows up as a community of souls is what we develop, in its childhood stage, in our working groups. What holds Eastern Europe so firmly to the group soul, causing it to regard the Slavic group soul as something that it does not want to abandon but, on the contrary, regards as a principle for the whole development of the state—it is this that must be overcome...

So this fifth post-Atlantean epoch of civilization needs what we develop and cultivate in our groups. It needs the conscious cultivation of the spiritual aura that still hovers above us, cherished by the spirits of the Higher Hierarchies, and that will flow into the souls of human beings when they live in the sixth epoch. It is not our way to turn as in Eastern Europe to the group soul life that is dead, to a form of community that is a mere survival of the old. Our efforts are to cherish and cultivate a living reality from its childhood— such is the community of our groups. It is not our way to look for what speaks in the blood, calling together only those who have blood in common, and to cultivate this in community. Our aim is to call together human beings who resolve to be brothers and sisters, and above whom hovers something that they strive to develop by cultivating spiritual science, feeling the good spirit of brotherhood hovering over and above them.

At the opening of one of our groups, this is the dedicatory thought we will receive into ourselves: Hereby we consecrate a group at its founding. Community and quickening life! We seek for community above us, the living Christ in us, the Christ who needs no document nor has first to be authenticated because we experience Him within ourselves. At the foundation of a group we will take this as our motto of consecration. 'Community above us; Christ in us.' We know furthermore that if two, or three, or seven, or many are united in this sense in the name of Christ, the Christ lives in them in very truth. All those who in this sense acknowledge Christ as their Brother, are themselves sisters and brothers. The Christ will recognize as His brother that person who recognizes other people as brothers.

If we are able to receive such words of consecration and carry on our work in accordance with them, the true spirit of our Movement will hold sway in whatever we do. Even in these difficult times, friends from outside have associated themselves with those who have founded the group here. This is always a good custom, for thereby those who are working in other groups are able to carry to other places the words of consecration. They pledge themselves to think constantly of those who have undertaken in a group to work together in accordance with the true spirit of the Movement. The invisible community, which we should like to found through the manner of our work, will thus grow and prosper. If this attitude, uniting with our work, becomes more and more widespread, we shall put to good account the demands made by spiritual science for the sake of the progress of mankind. Then we may believe that those great masters of wisdom who guide human progress and human knowledge will be with us. To the extent to which you here work in the sense of spiritual science, to that extent I know full well that the great masters who guide our work from the spiritual worlds will be in the midst of your labours.

7. The Michael Imagination: the Angel of Humanity

Humanity is not alone—though how often, in our freedom, we feel we stand alone! The powers of world evolution which make known to us the direction and meaning of our lives have always been represented under the term 'angels', messengers. Sometimes they have a special role, notably at turning-points like the present, where many people rightly begin to ask questions about the future development that can begin in a new cycle, and many people also have the sense of angelic communication. In a wider sense, we are in reality ourselves part of the rhythmic unfolding of the world, and are able to work with the angels in freedom in the cycle which is described as the 'Age of Michael'.

Michael is, according to Rudolf Steiner, the angel or archangel who eternally represents the very spiritual struggle which we must undertake at this phase of our evolution: the fight to master ahrimanic powers, the powers that would dehumanize us. In the biblical vision of the Apocalypse it was represented as Michael's fight with the Dragon, the 'ancient Snake' who was cast out of heaven. Later, the cosmic struggle was brought down to earth in the legends of St George. If anything can serve as an imaginative picture to inspire the present age, it is the Michael imagination. But if it is to continue to inspire us, it must also take deeper forms. The Dragon is manifest in the ahrimanic intelligence which nowadays assumes the most subtle guises; Michael does not repudiate intelligence, but stands for an intelligence that is at the same time a creative force in the world. Ultimately this creative intelligence will be ours as human beings, or rather as the 'Tenth Hierarchy' of cosmic powers ourselves. We will be able to share in it because the angelic power, the guardian of cosmic-creative thought, who has the name Michael, was also willing to share our human struggle towards higher consciousness. That is at the same time our struggle, within a spiritually dynamic universe, to be free.

It is possible to follow the progress of mankind from the point of view of man himself, from the stage of consciousness in which he felt himself as a member of the divine-spiritual order up to the present time, when he is conscious of himself as an individual, freed from the divine-spiritual and able to think for himself. In our last study this point of view was taken.

But it is also possible, through supersensible vision, to make a picture of what Michael and those who belong to him experience during this evolutionary process, i.e. to describe the facts of it as they appear to Michael himself. This shall now be attempted.

There is the earliest epoch in evolution, where it is only possible to speak of what takes place among divine-spiritual beings. Here one has to deal with the actions of the gods alone. Gods fulfil what the impulses of their natures inspire, and are satisfied in this their activity. Only what they themselves experience in all this is important. But in one corner of this field of the gods' activity something resembling mankind is to be observed, as forming a part of their divine activity.

The spiritual being who from the beginning directed his gaze towards mankind is Michael. He so orders the divine activities that in one part of the cosmos mankind may exist. And his own activity is of the same nature as that which is revealed later in man as intellect; but this intellect is active as a force that streams through the cosmos, ordering ideas and giving rise to actual realities. In this force Michael works. His office is to rule the cosmic intellectuality. And he wills the further progress in his domain, which consists in this: that that which works as intelligence throughout the whole cosmos should later become concentrated within the human individuality. As a result the following takes place: there comes a time in the evolution of the world when the cosmos subsists no longer in its own present intelligence, but on the cosmic intelligence belonging to the past. For the present intelligence must then be sought in the stream of human evolution.

What Michael desires is to keep the intelligence, which is developing within humanity, permanently in connection with the divine-spiritual beings.

But in this he is meeting with opposition. What the gods accomplish in their evolution, in that they release the cosmic intellectuality so that it may become a part of human nature, stands revealed as a fact within the world. If there are beings with power to perceive this fact, then they can take advantage of it. And such beings do indeed exist. They are the ahrimanic beings. It is their nature to absorb into themselves all that comes forth from the gods as intelligence. They have the capacity to unite with their own being the sum-total of all intellectuality, and thus they become the greatest, the most comprehensive and penetrating intelligences in the cosmos.

Michael foresees how man, in progressing more and more towards his own individual use of intelligence, must meet with these ahrimanic beings, and how by uniting with them he may then succumb to them. For this reason Michael brings the ahrimanic powers under his feet; he continually thrusts them into a deeper region than the one in which man is evolving. Michael thrusting the dragon at his feet into the abyss—that is the mighty picture which lives in human consciousness of the supersensible facts described here.

Evolution progresses. The intellectuality which was at first entirely in the sphere of divine spirituality detaches itself so far that it becomes the element that ensouls the cosmos. That which previously had only radiated from the gods themselves now shines as the manifestation of the divine from the world of the stars. Formerly the world had been guided by the divine being himself; it is now guided by the divine manifestation which has become objective, and behind this manifestation the divine being passes through the next stage of his own development.

Michael is again the ruler of the cosmic intelligence, in so far as this streams through the manifestations of the cosmos in the order of ideas.

The third phase of evolution is a further separation of the cosmic intelligence from its origin. In the worlds of the stars the present order of ideas no longer holds sway as the divine manifestation; the stars move and are regulated according to the order of ideas implanted in them in the past. Michael sees how the cosmic intellectuality, which he has hitherto ruled in the cosmos, proceeds on its way to earthly humanity.

But Michael also sees how the danger of humanity succumbing to the ahrimanic powers grows greater and greater. He knows that *as regards himself* he will always have Ahriman under his feet; but will it also be the case with man?

Michael sees the greatest event in the earth's history taking place. From the kingdom served by Michael himself Christ descends to the sphere of the earth, so as to be there when the intelligence is wholly with the human individuality. For man will then feel most strongly the impulse to devote himself to the power which has made itself fully and completely into the vehicle of intellectuality. But Christ will be there; through His great sacrifice He will live in the same sphere in which Ahriman also lives. Man will be able to choose between Christ and Ahriman. The world will be able to find the Christ-way in the evolution of humanity.

That is Michael's cosmic experience with that which he has to govern in the cosmos. In order to remain with that which he has to govern, he enters upon the path that leads from the cosmos to humanity. He has been on this path since the eighth century AD, but he really only took up his earthly office, into which his cosmic office has been changed, in the last third of the nineteenth century.

Michael cannot force human beings to do anything. For it is just through intelligence having come entirely into the sphere of the human individuality that compulsion has ceased. But in the supersensible world first bordering on this visible world, Michael can unfold as a majestic, exemplary action that which he wishes to display. He can show himself there with an aura of light, with the gesture of a spirit-being, in which all the splendour and glory of the past intelligence of the gods is revealed. He can there show how the action of this intelligence of the past is more true, more beautiful and more virtuous in the present than all that is contained in the immediate intelligence of the present day, which streams to us from Ahriman in deceptive, misleading splendour. He can point out how for him Ahriman will always be the lower spirit, under his feet.

Those persons who can see the supersensible world bordering next to the visible world perceive Michael and those belonging to him in the manner here described, engaged in what they would like to do for humanity. Such persons see how—through the picture of Michael in Ahriman's sphere— man is to be led in freedom away from Ahriman to Christ. When through their vision such persons also succeed in opening the hearts and minds of others, so that there is a circle of people who know how Michael is now living among mankind, humanity will then begin to celebrate festivals of Michael which will possess the right contents, and at which souls will allow the power of Michael to revive in them.

Michael will then work as a real power among mankind. People will be free and yet proceed along his spiritual path of life through the cosmos in intimate companionship with Christ.

Aphoristic Summary-Thoughts

To become truly conscious of the working of Michael in the spiritual order of the world is to solve the riddle of human freedom in relation to the cosmos, in so far as the solution is necessary for mankind on earth.

For 'Freedom' as a fact is directly given to every human being who understands himself in the present period of mankind's evolution. No one can say, 'Freedom is not,' unless he wishes to deny a patent fact. But we can find a certain contradiction between this fact of our experience and the processes of the cosmos. In contemplating the mission of Michael within the cosmos this contradiction is dissolved.

In my book *The Philosophy of Freedom** (The Philosophy of Spiritual Activity) the 'Freedom' of the human being in the present world-epoch is proved as an essential element of consciousness. In the descriptions here given of the mission of Michael, the cosmic foundations of the 'coming-into-being' of this Freedom are disclosed.

How then does man stand today in his present stage of evolution with respect to Michael and his hosts?

Man is surrounded today by a world which was once of a wholly divine-spiritual nature—divine-spiritual being of

---

* See Rudolf Steiner, *The Philosophy of Freedom*, trans. Michael Wilson (London 1999).

Rudolf Steiner and Clara Rettich, Michael and the Dragon *(apoc-alyptic seal). The 'Michael Imagination', intimated in the Book of Revelation, is connected by Rudolf Steiner with the spiritual struggle of our time in particular, and is in itself an inspiring power in the inner life. He describes Michael as the Angel of Humanity, and as guardian of cosmic, creative intelligence.*

which he also was a member. Thus at that time the world belonging to man was a world of divine-spiritual being. But this was no longer so in a later stage of evolution. The world had then become a cosmic manifestation of the divine-spiritual; the divine being hovered behind the manifestation. Nevertheless, the divine-spiritual lived and moved in all that was thus manifested. A world of stars was already there, in the light and movement of which the divine-spiritual lived and moved and manifested itself. One may say that at that time, in the position or movement of a star, the activity of the divine and spiritual was directly evident.

And in all this—in the working of the divine spirit in the cosmos, and in the life of man resulting from this divine activity—Michael was as yet in his own element, unhindered, unresisted. The adjustment of the relation between the divine and the human was in his hands.

But other ages dawned. The world of the stars ceased to be a direct and present manifestation of divine-spiritual activity. The constellations lived and moved, maintaining what the divine activity had been in them in the past. The divine-spiritual dwelt in the cosmos in manifestation no longer, but in the manner of its working only. There was now a certain distinct separation between the divine-spiritual and the cosmic world. Michael, by virtue of his own nature, adhered to the divine-spiritual, and endeavoured to keep mankind as closely as possible in touch with it.

This he continued to do, more and more. His will was to preserve man from living too intensely in a world which represents only the working of the divine and spiritual— which is not the real being, nor its manifestation.

It is a deep source of satisfaction to Michael that through man himself he has succeeded in keeping the world of the stars in direct union with the divine and spiritual. For when man, having fulfilled his life between death and a new birth, enters on the way to a new earth-life, in his descent he seeks to establish a harmony between the course of the stars and his coming life on earth. In olden times this harmony existed as a matter of course, because the divine-spiritual was active in the stars, where human life too had its source. But today, when the course of the stars is only a continuing of the manner in which the divine-spiritual worked in the past, this harmony cannot exist unless man seeks it. Man brings his divine-spiritual portion—which he has preserved from the past—into relation with the stars, which now only bear their divine-spiritual nature within them as an after-working from an earlier time.

In this way there comes into man's relation to the world something of the divine, which corresponds to former ages and yet appears in these later times. *That this is so is the deed of Michael.* And this deed gives him such deep satisfaction that in it he finds a portion of his very life, a portion of his sunlike, living energy.

But at the present time, when Michael directs his spiritual eyes to the earth, he sees another fact as well—very different from the above. During his physical life between birth and death man has a world around him in which even the *working* of the divine-spiritual no longer appears directly, but only something which has remained over as its result; we may describe it by saying it is only the accomplished work of the divine-spiritual. This accomplished work, in all its forms, is essentially of a divine and spiritual kind. To human vision the divine is manifested in the forms and in the processes of nature; but it is *no longer* indwelling as a living principle. Nature is this divinely accomplished work of God; nature everywhere around us is an image of the divine working.

In this world of sunlike divine glory, but no longer livingly divine, man dwells. Yet as a result of Michael's working upon him man has maintained his connection with the essential being of the divine and spiritual. He lives as a being permeated by God in a world that is no longer permeated by God.

Into this world that has become empty of God, man will carry what is in him—what his being has become in this present age.

Humanity will evolve into a new world evolution. The divine and spiritual from which man originates can become the cosmically expanding human being, radiating with a new light through the cosmos which now exists only as an image of the divine and spiritual.

The divine being which will thus shine forth through humanity will no longer be the same divine being which was once the cosmos. In its passage through humanity the divine-spiritual will come to a realization of being which it could not manifest before.

The ahrimanic powers try to prevent evolution from taking the course here described. It is not their will that the original divine-spiritual powers should illumine the universe in its further course. They want the cosmic intellectuality which they themselves have absorbed to radiate through the whole of the new cosmos, and in this intellectualized and ahrimanized cosmos they want man to continue to live.

Were he to live such a life man would lose Christ. For Christ came into the world with an intellectuality that is still of the very same essence as once lived in the divine-spiritual, when the divine-spiritual in its own being still informed the cosmos. But if at the present time we speak in such a manner that our thoughts can also be the thoughts of Christ, we set over against the ahrimanic powers something which can save us from succumbing to them.

To understand the meaning of Michael's mission in the cosmos is to be able to speak in this way. In the present time we must be able to speak of nature in the way demanded by the evolutionary stage of the consciousness soul, or spiritual soul. We must be able to receive into ourselves the purely natural-scientific way of thinking. But we ought also to learn to feel and speak about nature in a way that is according to Christ. We ought to learn the Christ-language—not only about redemption from nature, about the soul and things divine—but about the things of the cosmos.

When with inward, heartfelt feeling we realize the mission and the deeds of Michael and those belonging to him, when we enter into all that they are in our midst, then we shall be able to maintain our human connection with the divine and spiritual origin, and understand how to cultivate the Christ-language about the cosmos. For to understand Michael is to find the way in our time to the Logos, as lived by Christ here on earth and among human beings.

Anthroposophy truly values what the natural-scientific way of thinking has learned to say about the world during the last four or five centuries. But in addition to this language it speaks another, about the nature of man, about his evolution and that of the cosmos; for it would speak the language of Christ and Michael.

If both these languages are spoken it will not be possible for evolution to be broken off or to pass over to Ahriman before the original divine-spiritual is found. To speak only in the natural-scientific way corresponds to the separation of intellectuality from the original divine and spiritual. This *can* indeed lead over in the ahrimanic realm if Michael's mission remains unobserved. But *it will not do so* if through the power of Michael's example the intellect which has become free finds itself again in the original cosmic intellectuality, which has separated from man and become objective to him. For that cosmic intellectuality lies in the original source of man, and it appeared in Christ in full reality of being within the sphere of humanity, after it had left man for a time so that he might unfold his freedom.

Aphoristic Summary-Thoughts

The divine-spiritual comes to expression in the cosmos in different ways, in succeeding stages: (1) through its own and inmost *being*; (2) through the *manifestation* of this being; (3) through the *active working*, when the being withdraws from the manifestation; (4) through the *accomplished work*, when in the outwardly apparent universe no longer the divine itself but only the forms of the divine are there.

In the modern conception of nature man has no relation to the divine, but only to the accomplished work. With all that is imparted to the human soul by this science of nature, man can unite himself either with the powers of Christ or with the dominions of Ahriman.

Michael is filled with the striving—working through his example in perfect freedom—to embody in human cosmic evolution the relation to the cosmos which is still preserved in man himself from the ages when the divine being and the divine manifestation held sway. In this way, all that is said by the modern view of nature—relating as it does purely to the image, purely to the form of the divine—will merge into a higher, spiritual view of nature. The latter will indeed exist in man; but it will be an echo in human experience of the divine relation to the cosmos which prevailed in the first two stages of cosmic evolution. This is how anthroposophy confirms the view of nature which the age of the consciousness soul has evolved, while bringing to it that which is revealed to spiritual seership.

Sources

The lectures and writings by Rudolf Steiner are reproduced here in English versions, with occasional slight adaptations. For current editions see Further Reading list on page 135.

1. 'A Spiritual Perspective': extracts from lectures 1 and 2 (3–4 April 1912) of the lecture course published as *Spiritual Beings in the Heavenly Bodies and in the Kingdoms of Nature*, translator unknown (Steiner Book Centre, N. Vancouver 1981).
2. 'The Turn of the Millennium': extracts from lectures 1 and 2 (1–2 November 1919) of the lecture course published as *The Influences of Lucifer and Ahriman*, translated by D.S. Osmond (Rudolf Steiner Publishing Co., London 1954).
3. 'The Etheric or Life-sphere and the New Awareness of Christ': extract from a lecture (25 January 1910) published in the collection *The True Nature of the Second Coming*, translated by D.S. Osmond and C. Davy (Anthroposophical Publishing Co., London 1961).
4. 'Building for the Future: The Rediscovery of Form': extract from lectures (June 1914) from the course published as *Architecture as a Synthesis of the Arts*, translated by J. Collis (Rudolf Steiner Press, London 1999).
5. 'Educating for the Future: Love and Knowledge in the Waldorf School': extract from lecture 1 (17 July 1924) of the course published as *Human Values in Education*, translated by V. Compton-Burnett (Rudolf Steiner Press, London 1971).
6. 'Working with the Future': extract from a lecture (15 June 1915) published as *Preparing for the Sixth Epoch*, translator unknown (Anthroposophic Press, New York 1957).
7. 'The Michael Imagination: the Angel of Humanity': unabridged reproduction of essays by Rudolf Steiner together with the summary 'Leading Thoughts', nos. 109–114 on which they are a commentary, published in *Anthroposophical Leading Thoughts*, translated by G. and M. Adams (Rudolf Steiner Press, London 1973).

Further Reading

Books by Rudolf Steiner:

Angels (Rudolf Steiner Press 1998)
Anthroposophical Leading Thoughts (Rudolf Steiner Press 1998)
The Archangel Michael (Anthroposophic Press 1994)
Architecture as a Synthesis of the Arts (Rudolf Steiner Press 1999)
Art as Seen in the Light of Mystery Wisdom (Rudolf Steiner Press 1996)
The Education of the Child (Anthroposophic Press 1996)
Evil (Rudolf Steiner Press 1997)
The Evolution of Consciousness (Rudolf Steiner Press 1991)
The Fifth Gospel (Rudolf Steiner Press 1998)
The Influences of Lucifer and Ahriman (Anthroposophic Press 1993)
A Modern Art of Education (Rudolf Steiner Press 1972)
Nature Spirits (Rudolf Steiner Press 1995)
Self-Transformation (Rudolf Steiner Press 1995)
The Spiritual Beings in the Heavenly Bodies and in the Kingdoms of Nature (Anthroposophic Press 1992)
The Spiritual Hierarchies and the Physical World (Anthroposophic Press 1996)

Books by other authors:

Art Inspired by Rudolf Steiner, J. Fletcher (Mercury Arts Publications 1987)
Eloquent Concrete, R. Raab, A. Klingborg, A. Fant (Rudolf Steiner Press 1979)
The Goetheanum, H. Biesantz, A. Klingborg (Rudolf Steiner Press 1979)
The Language of Colour in the First Goetheanum, Hilde Raske (Verlag Freies Geistesleben 1983)
Rudolf Steiner's Sculpture in Dornach, A. Fant, A. Klingborg, J. Wilkes (Rudolf Steiner Press 1975)

Publisher's Note Regarding
Rudolf Steiner's Lectures

The lectures and addresses contained in this volume have been translated from the German, which is based on stenographic and other recorded texts that were in most cases never seen or revised by the lecturer. Hence, due to human errors in hearing and transcription, they may contain mistakes and faulty passages. Every effort has been made to ensure that this is not the case. Some of the lectures were given to audiences more familiar with anthroposophy; these are the so-called 'private' or 'members' lectures. Other lectures, like the written works, were intended for the general public. The difference between these, as Rudolf Steiner indicates in his *Autobiography*, is twofold. On the one hand, the members' lectures take for granted a background in and commitment to anthroposophy; in the public lectures this was not the case. At the same time, the members' lectures address the concerns and dilemmas of the members, while the public work speaks directly out of Steiner's own understanding of universal needs. Nevertheless, as Rudolf Steiner stresses: 'Nothing was ever said that was not solely the result of my direct experience of the growing content of anthroposophy. There was never any question of concessions to the prejudices and preferences of the members. Whoever reads these privately printed lectures can take them to represent anthroposophy in the fullest sense. Thus it was possible without hesitation—when the complaints in this direction became too persistent—to depart from the custom of circulating this material "for members only". But it must be borne in mind that faulty passages do occur in these reports not revised by myself.' Earlier in the same chapter, he states: 'Had I been able to correct them [the private lectures], the restriction *for members only* would have been unnecessary from the beginning.'